The Private MAJOR

JOHN MAJOR
At home in Huntingdon
by DEBBIE DAVIES

The **Hunts Post**

THE PRIVATE MAJOR

It would not have been possible to write, or complete this book without the support and encouragement of my partner Terry and the understanding and patience of my children Martin, Aaron and Russell.
I would like to thank everyone who made a contribution to this book, giving me the chance to meet some interesting people and fulfil a life-time's ambition.

Special thanks go to John and Norma Major who agreed to be interviewed at short notice.
My colleagues Paul Richardson (*Hunts Post* editor), who also edited this book, Marcus Crawley and Annalise Pavitt, who took on some of my work during the last few weeks of writing this book, and Helen Drake for her excellent photographs.

My only intention in writing this book was to add some colour to the dull picture that has often been painted of John Major.

Debbie Davies, October 1997

First published in 1997 by *The Hunts Post*

Typeset in Nimrod
Printed and bound by BPC Wheatons Ltd, Exeter
ISBN 0-9502952-3-X

Contents

THE PRIVATE MAJOR

Foreword

E VER since I was selected as the prospective Conservative candidate for the Huntingdon Parliamentary Constituency 20 years ago, this has been our home. Living previously in Hemingford Grey and now Great Stukeley, I can think of nowhere else in England that I would rather live.

As a family, we have made countless friends and have enjoyed being part of the local community. I intend that this will remain so both during and after the time I am Member of Parliament.

Huntingdonshire comprises a large number of communities, be they towns or villages. Each has its own identity and special features, but together they form a unique part of our country.

During the past two decades we have seen many changes. The local economy in this part of Cambridgeshire has grown enormously. Increased employment prospects have encouraged more people to more into the area. Local councillors have worked with dedication to take every possible step to ensure a balanced planning policy to protect our environment and a sense of balance between old and new.

I am very proud to have represented this constituency for the past 18 years. This book is the culmination of an historic period in our local life. I would like to thank *The Hunts Post* for originating the idea and wish it every success.

**The Right
Honourable
John Major MP,
October 1997**

THE PRIVATE MAJOR

GREEN FIELDS

As Norma Major drove up the A1 towards Huntingdon on a damp November afternoon in 1976, she turned to her husband and asked if he realised the significance of the day. Concerned that he had forgotten an important anniversary, John Major hesitated before admitting that he didn't.

She steered their battered brown Mini around the Buckden roundabout and told him November 19 was exactly five years to the day that he had been selected to represent the Conservative Party as a Prospective Parliamentary Candidate for St Pancras North. Norma believed the coincidence was a good sign and meant he would be successful that night.

In the past few weeks they had made the long journey to Huntingdon from their home in Beckenham, Kent, several times. John had applied to be the next Conservative Parliamentary candidate for Huntingdon and had to attend several interviews and a cocktail party as part of the selection procedure.

He was well prepared. On earlier visits he and Norma had taken the time to look around the constituency and meet local people, and they were now familiar with all the signposts for the little villages dotted along the A1.

Despite strong competition for one of the safest Conservative seats in the country and some bad luck, John had reached the final stage of the selection process and he and Norma were on their way to the Commemoration Hall in Huntingdon.

THE PRIVATE MAJOR

He had to make a speech, and then a general meeting of association and party members would decide who would succeed Sir David Renton. Norma was confident it would be her husband. John recalled:

"When the vacancy popped through the letterbox at Beckenham, Norma had a premonition that I would be selected. Norma knew this part of the world very well because as a child she spent the summer holidays in Bourn, just outside the constituency. It was just her mother and Norma then and her mother had to work, so Norma came down to stay in the holidays."

Although John trusted Norma's intuition about the evening's events, there had been many occasions in recent years when he had doubted whether he would fulfil his ambition to enter the House of Commons.

He joined Brixton Young Conservatives in 1960, aged 16, when a canvasser knocked on the door of the home he shared with his parents Tom and Gwen, brother Terry and sister Pat.

But his dream to be part of the great British institution was hatched much earlier on a visit to Westminster. As a 13-year-old schoolboy he looked around the great meeting rooms and observed the proceedings in awe, determined, one day, to take his place on the benches.

An interest in the political system, a dream of becoming an MP and being a fully-paid up member of a political party are all pointers to a career in politics, but there are strict rules governing the Conservative Party's list of potential MPs.

The system has changed over the years, but in the early seventies, John needed to be approved by Central Office before his name could be added to the Candidates' List, which was then sent out to constituencies where there were vacancies for MPs.

It is essential for all potential candidates to have an appropriate career and they need to find a Conservative MP to sponsor them.

10

His job at the Standard Chartered Bank in London – he joined in September, 1966 – was progressing well. His stint in the Young Conservative movement in Brixton, where he served as treasurer, vice chairman, political officer and chairman, was essential for his CV. As was his local council experience.

In 1964 he represented the Conservatives in the Lambeth Borough Council elections for the Larkhall ward, a Labour stronghold, but failed to be elected. His first political breakthrough came in May, 1968, when he was elected as a Conservative councillor for Ferndale, a ward of Lambeth Borough Council.

Although his success was short-lived, John was appointed vice chairman and later chairman of housing, gaining some invaluable experience on the borough's council estates.

It was as chairman of housing that John met Peter Brown, the man who was to become his constituency agent in Huntingdon some 15 year later. Peter was Conservative agent for the Norwood constituency. He said:

"I remember our first meeting very well. It was in his office at the town hall and I was impressed by his remarkably mercurial political brain. You couldn't help make a mental note of him. He was clearly one of the outstanding political youngsters of the time; someone who had a lot to contribute."

Labour swept the board at the local elections in May, 1971, ousting most of the Lambeth Conservative councillors. But the remainder of the year proved to be fruitful for the Majors. Jill Knight, MP for Birmingham Edgbaston, agreed to sponsor John and he was accepted on the Candidates' List and invited to apply for selection to St Pancras North. In November of that year Norma gave birth to a baby girl, who they named Elizabeth.

As prospective Parliamentary candidate for St Pancras North, again a staunch Labour area, John fought two unsuccessful elections in February and October, 1974.

THE PRIVATE MAJOR

Afterwards, in despondent mood, he decided he would only accept interviews for constituencies where he at least had a chance of being elected, should he be selected.

Although his CV was widely circulated, he was turned down by Portsmouth North, Norwood and Paddington. Then, in 1976, he received a telephone call from an old friend and former agent, Jean Lucas, who wanted to know why he had not included his local council experience on his CV.

When he told her he had, she made some checks and found out that for the past 12 months Central Office had been sending out the wrong CV to constituencies all over the country. Incredibly, there were two John Majors on the Candidates' List, the other was GLC candidate.

It was not surprising that he could not even get an interview. No-one knew about his diligent work for the housing department in the tough, multi-cultural borough of Lambeth. In fact, three years later, it was his local council experience and knowledge of housing problems on the large London council estates which most impressed some members of the Huntingdon selection committee. Others were more concerned with what he knew about farming.

Roger Juggins, a Great Stukeley farmer and manager of Huntingdon Racecourse, who was chairman of Huntingdon Conservative Club at that time, had been chosen to serve on the committee to test the candidates' knowledge of agriculture and rural life.

When John attended the first interview, hands nervously clasped in his lap, it would have been safe to assume that the willowy 33-year-old banker in his pin-striped suit, with his large spectacles and south London accent, probably didn't even own a pair of wellingtons, but Roger had a job to do. He said:

"My questions were the farming questions and I wanted to know what their attitude was to country sports.

12

THE PRIVATE MAJOR

"The Wilson Government was stirring up the anti brigade at that time, so I asked John Major what he thought about country sports. He looked at me and said: 'cricket, football'? He hadn't come in contact with these things, but why should he?

"He said he had nothing against country sports in principle and promised to do some research on it. It was the same with farming. He admitted that he knew nothing about farming, but neither did Lord Renton and within six months he knew everything about it and it was the same with John. We didn't expect him to know how to calf cows, we just wanted him to get into the politics."

The most difficult task for all the selection committee members was trying to find a candidate who could follow in the footsteps of Sir David Renton, knighted in 1965, who served as Huntingdon's MP for 34 years.

His impeccable background, distinguished army record and devotion to his family and the people of Huntingdon made him a well-respected local figure.

He and his wife Paddy had raised thousands of pounds for several charities, including the Mencap charity, of which he was president, and worked tirelessly in the constituency. Many felt he would be hard, if not impossible, to replace.

The late Commander Archie Gray was chairman of the Conservative Association in early 1976 when David Renton announced that he would not be standing at the next election.

Commander Gray said at the time:

"He has been a superb MP and I just hope we can, in due course, find a successor who matches up to his qualities."

There was no shortage of interest for the safe Tory shire seat, with its historic connections to Oliver Cromwell and Samuel Pepys.

The original list of 300 applicants makes interesting reading now. At the time, the selection committee had no qualms about discarding the names of Chris Patten, Peter

Lilley, Michael Howard and Peter Brooke.

Because of the large number of applicants, Commander Gray decided to split the committee, which was made up of local association and party members and some county county councillors, into three groups.

They met at The Views in George Street, Huntingdon, which was then the headquarters of the Conservative Club and Association.

As they sat round a large oak table in a room on the top floor of the red brick Victorian house, the former home of a Harold Clayton, and waded through the huge pile of CVs night after night they were reminded by Commander Gray to keep one eye on the future. Roger Juggins said:

"We met at The Views at 6.30pm on the Friday night and worked all day Saturday and most of Sunday, finishing at 8pm on Sunday.

"Our first job was to sort out all the applications into A, B and C material. On the second weekend we had the Bs and the Cs from the other two groups and picked out what we considered to be any A material from those.

"It took three weekends to finally get it down to 32. Archie Gray had told us to look for a possible Cabinet minister. He said we had a prime seat, close to London, which had always been Tory. It was an ideal position for a Cabinet minister.

"The following weekend we threw a cocktail party, when the 32 applicants and their wives were invited.

"We made a point that the wife had to be there. Wives are important . . . well they are in the Huntingdon constituency. We interviewed them all that weekend and came up with four."

They were: the Marquess of Douro, who was heir to the eighth Duke of Wellington, two former MPs, Jock Bruce Gardyne and Alan Haselhurst, and John Major.

John had won a lot of people over with his straightforward attitude and astute political brain, but some of the association members let it be known that they would prefer to have the titled Marquess representing Huntingdon or the experienced Mr Gardyne or Mr

Haselhurst.

In the end, even the traditionalists had to admit that John's local council experience and knowledge of Londoners would be a real asset in an area where half the population were now newcomers displaced from the capital.

Then there was Norma. Many felt this quiet, shy, former school teacher was perfect for the task ahead and the couple were keen to move to the area, should John be selected, which was something the committee were insisting on anyway. Huntingdon MPs have always lived in the constituency.

One of the most sceptical members of the committee was Jo Johnson, who was president of the association. She and John were to become great friends in time before her death in September 1993, but at those first few meetings she couldn't help feeling he was: "just a bit too clever."

Jo, a no-nonsense Scots lady, was the wise old owl of the committee and prided herself on being a good judge of character. A few days before the voting took place, she confided her fears to Emily Blatch, now Lady Blatch:

"The first thing Jo said to me about the final list of candidates was that there was this man called John Major and she said the trouble is we're stuck between thinking: 'Is he is too clever by half or is he for real'?

"It seemed that he was able to respond to any question. He appeared to be a man of detail, but also a man who was capable of thinking strategically.

"Part of the process is actually to catch people out and put them under a lot of pressure. They are given assignments to do and speeches to make at short notice – that kind of thing – to see how they respond and react. So when I first met him, just before he was selected, I was looking out for that and always trying to work out if this man was for real.

"My first impression was that he was very warm and had a very good rapport with a room full of strangers, but he was incredibly good at taking any issue and talking about it in some detail and then taking it forward to where it fitted strategically in the scheme of things. I

THE PRIVATE MAJOR

remember thinking, Jo had got it right, but I think he is for real. He's genuine."

All the prospective candidates had to give a speech on the final night. The order was drawn by lot and John was last. He stood on the stage at the Commemoration Hall in Huntingdon's High Street before an enthralled audience of about 200 people and spoke with conviction, political foresight and passion. In 20 minutes he managed to home in on the things that were important to the people of Huntingdon as they approached a new decade.

Although Huntingdon was still regarded as a rural community, the demographics had changed dramatically in the previous decade.

The Oxmoor housing estate in the town centre of Huntingdon had been built in the late fifties as part of a Greater London Council's programme to find homes and jobs for the London overspill. New factories and industry, such as Myers Beds on the edge of the Oxmoor estate, provided work for the arrivals.

The population of the traditional market town of Huntingdon and nearby Godmanchester was 8821 in 1961 – 10 years later it had virtually doubled to 16,557.

Industry was also beginning to sprout up on the industrial estates on the outskirts of the town and the rail link through Huntingdon and St Neots made the area an ideal location for commuters.

The historic county of Huntingdonshire was dissolved on April 1, 1974. Huntingdonshire and the Soke of Peterborough were merged with Cambridgeshire and the Isle of Ely to form a new Cambridgeshire. Huntingdonshire County Council was replaced by a new district council, based in Huntingdon.

John's first impressions were of a rural area that was changing, and on those early visits to the town in 1976 he was surprised to find over half the population had moved in during the previous 10 years. He said:

"You could see the changing face of East Anglia from what was happening in Huntingdon. It was still perceived from outside as a very traditional rural seat, but it actually already had a very large commuter base that had moved in.

"It was evident from the sheer scale of people moving in that it was changing. What concerned me from the outset was not to put up a barrier and say nobody else should come in, because that was clearly not practical or necessarily even desirable because the newcomers were bringing prosperity, job opportunities and choice and development with them, but to make sure when they came in that two things happened. That they were assimilated and you didn't have two communities, a rural community and an incoming community gazing in hostile fashion at one another and to make sure that the development that took place didn't destroy the attractiveness of the constituency. It was an extremely attractive place. It had some beautiful villages with some lovely houses."

It was these sentiments and his pledge to learn whatever he needed to know about the local community which persuaded the general meeting of the association that John Major was the right man for the job.

Cyril Bridge, who ran a haulage business in the town and served on the district and county councils, says when he was asked to sit on the selection committee, he was concerned that no-one could measure up to Sir David Renton, but after meeting John and Norma he changed his mind. John's performance that night left him in no doubt that a suitable replacement had been found. He said:

"It wasn't difficult to pick John, it was easy. There was just something about the fella. A lot of us said: 'He's right for Huntingdon' and, of course, we were right.

"I can see him now walking onto that stage to give his speech. It's hard to describe, but there was something in that speech that people could beam in on and Norma she was like a bright light and has been all along. We knew she would make an ideal MP's wife."

While other members deliberated, John and Norma,

convinced there would be a second or even third ballot, decided to go outside and get some fresh air. As they walked back up the deserted High Street, they noticed someone standing at the door waving and motioning for them to hurry up.

Even before they reached the door, they could hear the applause. John was quickly ushered to the stage to deliver his acceptance speech.

There had been no need for a second ballot, he had won outright, with 60 per cent of the vote.

He composed himself and said: "It's a long way from the back streets of Brixton to the green fields of Huntingdon."

Deep down, he and Norma suspected the journey had only just begun.

RAINY DAY

J OHN and Norma Major had made a positive impression during the six months it took to select a new candidate, but some were still not sure about the newcomers.

Although he will be 90 in 1998, Lord Renton is still patron of the Conservative Party in Huntingdon, always ready with advice and wisdom.

Elected as MP for the Huntingdon constituency in 1945, his judgement would have carried a lot of weight, but he didn't think it would be right for him to be involved in the selection of his successor, so he took a trip to the United States of America.

When he learned the result from Andrew Thomson, the Conservative agent for Huntingdon until 1983, he was a little taken aback; but then he wasn't the only one. Andrew says:

"There was great surprise from outside that a banker from south London had been chosen, because most people still regarded it as a county seat. None of us knew what to expect, but we all liked John and felt he would do well."

So it was with mixed feelings and some anticipation that Lord Renton travelled to Huntingdon Town Hall in December, 1976.

He had heard so much about the new candidate, this man from the city who knew nothing about farming and country life, but today at the official adoption meeting he would finally be allowed to make up his own mind.

19

THE PRIVATE MAJOR

Lord Renton says:

"I liked him straight away, and Norma. When he gave his speech, he
spoke for nearly 20 minutes, without notes, and managed to
summarise the current political situation and say what should be done
about it. I was very impressed. I have never met a man with a finer
and quicker brain and better memory."

John and Norma became good friends with David and his
wife Paddy over the years, and often visited the Renton
family home in the pretty village of Abbots Ripton, which
flanks the Great River Ouse.

It was there over Saturday evening meals and Sunday
lunches that Norma's interest in the Mencap charity
began. Lady Paddy Clair Renton was an avid fundraiser.

The Rentons, who had a daughter Davina with mental and
physical disabilities themselves, were involved with
several charities. Paddy raised money for the Red Cross,
was president of the Greater London Association of
Disabled (GLAD) and supported her husband in his work
with Mencap. She died of cancer in 1986.

Lord Renton was a former chairman and president of the
Huntingdon branch of the charity. When she first became
involved with Mencap, Norma's aim was to sell as many
Christmas cards as she could each year. Over the years she
has organised hundreds of events, such as balls, antique
fairs and an annual cricket match in Huntingdon.

But it was as the wife of the current Prime Minister that
she was able to capitalise on her position and raise large
sums of money. She was able to raise thousands of pounds
from holding receptions at Downing Street and opera
evenings at Chequers, the Prime Minister's weekend
retreat.

Mencap's chairman Brian Rix once estimated that her
involvement was worth about £1 million a year. She is still
president of the Huntingdon branch, where members say
Norma's association has helped to provide two Mencap
homes. A third is being built.

THE PRIVATE MAJOR

Although Norma and John were desperate to settle down in Huntingdon, it was almost two years before they were able to sell their home in Beckenham, a situation which was frustrating and costly. In the 12 months it took them to find a suitable house, they visited the constituency as much as possible, sometimes staying over at weekends.

Eventually they bought a £17,500 modern detached house in Hemingford Grey, a quintessentially English village just outside Huntingdon with a medieval church, thatched cottages and a country pub, and moved in during the December of 1977, almost a year before the Beckenham house was sold. Daughter Elizabeth, now six, attended the village school and James, their son, went to the local playgroup.

John still had his job at the Standard Chartered Bank, where he ran the public relations department, and joined his fellow commuters on the platform of Huntingdon Station every week-day morning to catch the early train to Kings Cross.

It was standing on that platform day after day that made him appreciate that something had to be done about the rail service, which he says was still in the dark ages at that time.

British Rail was still using old rolling stock and the trains were slow and irregular and stopped too often. The area had a large commuter base and many young couples on the new housing estates in Huntingdon and St Neots, who still had extended families living in London, told him they were unable to visit their relatives because fares were so expensive. One of his first challenges, he decided, was to improve the lot of the area's rail travellers.

He wrote letters to British Rail, pointing out the inconvenient time-table and the uncomfortable journey.

With an election looming – early forecasts were for the autumn of 1978 – John had a lot of work to do in the constituency. The most vulnerable time for a new candidate is in the run-up to that first election; it's when the opposition are likely to take a swipe or bring in a strong candidate.

The time had come for John to meet the electorate and those around him at that time, the local association and party members, his foot soldiers as they like to be known, say he threw himself into the constituency.

He made his first public appearance under the watchful eye of Roger Juggins.

On May Bank Holiday Monday in 1977, Roger invited John and Norma to Huntingdon races. Roger says:

"It was a wonderful day, John walked around and shook hands with everybody, even the old boy who went around the parade ring clearing up the droppings. People never got over that. It didn't matter what their politics were . . . there were no barriers . . . he just shook hands with everybody that day."

But, as far as the electorate was concerned, John Major was still an unknown quantity. Lord Renton was so well loved and respected it was difficult to know how the banker from Brixton would be accepted. But he had gone through a vigorous process to be selected, against impressive competition, and now when he was so close, he wasn't about to lose. John said:

"I'd come from the inner cities where Conservatives didn't win seats. I wasn't about to lose one in Cambridgeshire.

"You don't follow a better predecessor than David Renton. His record in Huntingdon will never be matched. Nobody will ever serve 34 years as the Member of Parliament for Huntingdon and 50 years in Parliament. I don't think it can be done again.

"I wasn't trying to get a higher majority than David, particularly, there was no competition between us. He couldn't have been more supportive from the moment I came.

"He didn't force advice, just gave it when it was needed. But I did think we'd get a bigger majority because coming from outside the area I could see and know better than people who lived here the nature of the vote that was coming in and at the end of the seventies, it was a vote that had fled the big cities. People had suffered from the policies of the controlling parties in the cities, which were predominately Labour.

"So although many people here thought the newcomers would bring the Labour vote with them, I was pretty certain that they wouldn't and I was proved right.

In 1979 the constituency was much bigger than it is now. The electorate was a massive 93,862. It extended further north, up to the outskirts of the city of Peterborough and took in St Neots, which is the biggest town in Cambridgeshire to the south.

Some of the broader issues for the new candidate to contend with included the road network, which had failed to keep up with the pace of industry and the increased population. The M11 hadn't been built and much of the A1 hadn't been dualled. Hundreds of heavy lorries were thundering through villages like Kimbolton and Needingworth every day, which led to protests and calls for by-passes.

Farmers in the Fens had drainage problems, unemployment was rising and a new hospital was needed in the constituency. John also had a hint of urban problems in his green fields.

A story of teenage tramps being discovered sleeping rough in and around Huntingdon was reported in *The Hunts Post*. According to the newspaper, the youngsters were school leavers who were "on the dole and had domestic problems."

John had two ambitions for that first election. The first was to win. With two previous defeats in St Pancras North in 1974 he was determined to do well. The second was to nudge Lord Renton's previous 9250 majority over the 10,000 mark.

Nationally, the Labour Party was in crisis and served most of that last term with a minority Government. Margaret Thatcher had become the new leader of the Conservative Party in February, 1975.

As rubbish began piling up on the streets and teachers,

rail workers and other public sector workers continued to strike, the "winter of discontent" in 1978-9 convinced the British people that it was time for change.

The Labour Party had managed to fend off calls for an election in 1978, but lost a vote of confidence in the early spring of 1979. Polling day was set for May 3. The day of the announcement, March 29, was John's 36th birthday. He said at the time it was the best birthday present he'd ever had.

During that first election campaign, Lady Blatch, then a county councillor and later leader of Cambridgeshire County Council, got to know John better.

Lady Blatch was responsible for organising the postal votes system during the day and would go out canvassing in the evenings. She says there was a good team spirit and everyone worked hard:

"One day, John said to me: 'Emily you'll forgive me for being personal, but I've noticed that you're here all day and then at 6pm you go off and canvass. Don't you find that difficult?'
I said: 'Well first of all it's only for three weeks, but yes if it was for any longer I would find it difficult.' He said: 'But you have children of school age don't you? I'm sorry if I'm prying, but what happens to the children when you're not there?' I said: 'I have a wonderful lady at home called Mrs Irvine without whom I could do absolutely nothing. She really is my right hand and she knew when the election was called I would need as much time as possible to help. So for three weeks, she has been collecting the children from school and feeding them for me.'
"That was the end of the conversation and I thought nothing more about it. But, a few days later Mrs Irvine came rushing in and said, 'I've received this letter. It's from a Mr Major. It said: "Dear Mrs Irvine, you don't know me, my name's John Major, I am the prospective parliamentary candidate for Huntingdon. Emily is working for me during the campaign and I know if it wasn't for you she wouldn't be able to help and if it wasn't for her I wouldn't be able to win this election and I just wanted you to know how deeply grateful I am".'
"I thought 'wow', in the middle of this election he has taken the time to write a hand-written note to somebody. I have to say that at the

same time I also thought well, 'new broom', he's trying hard. But that story is all the more poignant today because you could say that about any new candidate, but he hasn't changed. It doesn't matter what he's doing or how busy he is, he will always take the time to write to people who are unwell or suffering in some way."

During the election campaign, John visited every town and almost every village in the constituency; he met thousands of people and gave hundreds of speeches. His campaign team say this is when he's at his best. He loves meeting people and manages to create an instant rapport with them, whatever their background.

Although he had refused to take the vote for granted there were some early signs of success on polling day. John says:

"On election day I was being driven round by Archie Gray and as we drove past a polling station in Brampton and saw people queuing to get in, Archie said: 'There's your majority. They are not queuing to vote the present Government back in.' So we reached for the picnic basket and had a very early drink."

Even so, he did have some last minute doubts. Lady Blatch says:

"When it came to the count, he was completely neurotic. He wouldn't believe he had won. I said to him: 'They've counted the Labour vote and they've counted the Liberal vote and they're still adding ours to the tables, but he just said: 'Yes, but there might be some missing boxes'.

"He did that at every single election. He never took anything for granted and every single time he was elected in Huntingdon he increased the majority until eventually he had the biggest majority of any Conservative MP in the country. It meant a lot to him to win. This was his home and where he belonged and he wanted to do well."

As he stood on the balcony of the town hall in Huntingdon, where the result was declared, and waited for the returning officer to speak, his quiet optimism at last gave way to exhilaration. He knew for sure he was about to fulfil his ambition to take up his place in Parliament.

John, Norma and the rest of the campaign team were still on a high from the night before after hearing the news that Margaret Thatcher had become Britain's first woman Prime Minister.

There was tremendous excitement in Huntingdon. After five years of Labour rule John would not only take his place in the House of Commons, his Party would be forming the next Government.

When the announcement finally came at midday, he had done better than he or any of the campaign team could have ever imagined.

He had polled 40,193 votes, giving him a majority of 21,563. He told *The Hunts Post* he had expected to win, but not by such a large margin.

The Labour candidate Julian Fulbrooke said he was happy with his 18,630 vote, which increased his count by 800, but was convinced that the rain at tea time on polling day must have put some Labour voters off. He said:

"You never really know in organisational terms how much it costs you when it rains in the evening."

As John left the Labour candidate lamenting about the weather, he and Norma returned to Hemingford Grey where there was a bottle of Champagne chilling in the fridge. As they drove along the country roads, John was already making plans.

The day he had been dreaming about for so long had finally arrived. Norma said:

"I suppose we did not know what was ahead, but we knew we had taken a huge step somewhere in the right direction. John wanted to be an MP, he was the candidate and he had been successful. I think the limit of John's ambition then was to be Chancellor of the Exchequer. I think we see it as a little disappointing that he wasn't in that job a bit longer. But when other, bigger opportunities arise, you have to take them."

THE PRIVATE MAJOR

John said:

"I had just got into the House of Commons after wishing to be a Member of Parliament for 23 years. We had just gained a bigger majority than anyone could have imagined. I got home to my front door and there were all sorts of messages there – lucky black cats, bottles of Champagne and things like that which local people had placed there. It had been a hugely exciting day. I was also very tired . . . it had been a three-week election campaign with three public meetings each night and I'd been pretty busy during the day. The immediate excitement was going to the House of Commons, how your life was going to change. I was thinking: 'How are we going to manage with just the one beat-up old car'. . . ."

CHEAP WINE AND BAD CHEESE

ONCE the election was over, it was time for John and Norma Major to discuss practical arrangements. The Standard Chartered Bank had agreed to let him work part-time, but John was keen to make his mark on Westminster, which meant he would have to put in longer hours.

After much soul-searching they both agreed it would be better if Norma stayed in Hemingford Grey with the children, Elizabeth, who was now eight and James, aged four, during the week. John would travel to London on Monday morning, stay in a bedsit all week, and come home for the weekend. John said:

"We decided we wouldn't bundle up the family and leave the children unsettled, commuting from London and back again and being treated as having a walk-on part in our lives.

"In their interests, Norma would stay in Hemingford Grey and I would go to London on Monday and return on Thursday night or Friday morning. I had constituency work on Fridays and Saturdays and in those days I did a lot of Sunday mornings as well, with receptions and functions."

John had quickly gained the support and trust of the Party members in Huntingdon, but impressing his colleagues in Whitehall was bound to be more difficult.

It has often been said that John Major always seemed to be in the right place at the right time, but John Bridge, the current chairman of the Huntingdon Conservative Association argues:

28

"It always appeared that way, but I don't think the things he achieved in such a short space of time were by accident.

"He has the ability to recognise and the strategic skills to see where it is he needs to go and when he needs to be there.

"He has a tremendous political nose and a great capacity for work. He's able to grasp things rapidly and get down to the key issues and take quick and effective action."

So much so, that less than two years after arriving at Westminster, he was appointed Parliamentary Private Secretary to Home Office ministers Timothy Raisen and Patrick Mayhew.

The post gave him new challenges and a greater workload, but he was never allowed to forget the issues of the day back in his Huntingdon constituency.

As the relationship between the Soviet Union and the West became more fragmented, John and his agent Andrew Thomson received several phone calls and were even stopped in the street by constituents concerned about the future.

Huntingdon is surrounded by four airbases, two of which are American, set up after the second world war. RAF Alconbury is to the north-east of Huntingdon, close to the village of Great Stukeley, where John and Norma now live, and RAF Molesworth to the west of the town. Two British bases, RAF Wyton and RAF Brampton are on the outskirts of Huntingdon.

The decision in 1980 to station 64 cruise missiles at RAF Molesworth triggered seven years of conflict between peace protesters, security forces, the Government and local people.

By 1982, the tiny village of Molesworth had been besieged by peace campers, as many as 300 at any one time, who supported the Campaign for Nuclear Disarmament (CND).

Many people living in Molesworth and nearby Brington and Bythorn objected to having their rural peace shattered, whatever the laudable aims of the protesters, and set up a Ratepayers Against Molesworth Settlement group.

THE PRIVATE MAJOR

Although John understood people's fears about having so much weaponry in close proximity to their homes, in line with Conservative thinking he supported mutual disarmament and refused to meet the protesters.

Taking flak is an expected part of the job for anyone who embarks on a career in politics, but there was one occasion in 1982 when the bullets came a bit too close.

As one of 11 MPs on a fact-finding tour of the Middle East, John and the then Ipswich MP Ken Weetch came under fire in the town of Biet Ammar when fighting broke out between Arab and Israeli youths.

When asked later about the incident, he told a *Hunts Post* reporter how he had to dive for cover under the official car as he and Ken where caught in a hail of bricks and bullets.

John quipped:

"If they had come much closer there would have been a by-election in Huntingdon."

In January, 1983, Margaret Thatcher promoted John to the Whips' Office, appointing him junior whip. Of the Conservative backbenchers who came into Parliament at the 1979 election, he was one of only eight to be given a Government post. The move also made him one of the youngest members of the Government. This post, which he described at the time as "a leap one has to make", meant he had to give up his job at the bank due to Parliamentary regulations.

During the excitement of his promotion, and the pressures that created, both personally and professionally, John never neglected his Huntingdon constituency.

He maintains that his family, which he describes as pivotal to his career, his friendships with Party and association members and his contact with constituents, have all enabled him to keep his life in perspective.

The relationships he has with ordinary people are a constant reminder of where he belongs and why he chose a career in politics. He has always held regular constituency days, even when he became Prime Minister. On a typical day, he will visit a school or a factory in the morning and then hold an advice surgery, which is open for any resident of the constituency, in the afternoon. There is usually a function or dinner to attend in the evening. He refuses to let people down, no matter how tired he is. Roger Juggins says:

"There were times, especially during election campaigns, when I would say: 'John you don't have to do this one, we can go another time, they won't mind.' But he wouldn't hear of it. He would say: 'No, they're expecting me and will be disappointed if I don't turn up' . . . then fall asleep in the car on the way home."

By the time the 1983 election was announced in May for June 9, the boundaries of the constituency had changed, one of many alterations over the years.

The Boundary Commission redrew the constituency lines and robbed John Major and the Huntingdon seat of 20,000 potential voters. The largest percentage became part of the new South West Cambridgeshire seat, which took in St Neots and the surrounding villages.

Sir Anthony Grant was the Conservative's prospective parliamentary candidate brought in to fight that seat.

Several villages to the south of Peterborough were returned to the city. A plan to remove St Ives, Fenstanton and Needingworth from the Huntingdon constituency was rejected by the Boundary Commission after local people organised a campaign to fight the proposal.

It was during this election campaign that the later-to-be famous soapbox was introduced. John would make public speeches at market squares and shopping centres at the weekends. Without the support of his campaign team it would have been impossible for him to get around many village halls and committees in the constituency.

Sometimes there were two or three meetings to attend in an evening, so Lady Blatch would go to the second hall and deliver a warm-up speech while John was at the first, then while he was taking questions at the second venue, she would move on to the third gathering and present her piece again.

It was on one such occasion that John was reminded that not everyone in Huntingdon would be voting for him at the next election. Lady Blatch remembers:

"We were at a meeting on the Oxmoor estate and somebody in the audience started to get really rattled. So John stopped and addressed that one person. Instead of feeling all brave, the man suddenly started to look all embarrassed and as he stormed off out the room, he walked into a cupboard. The whole room just fell apart laughing.

"There were lots of fun moments like that. He loved a lively audience and didn't ever mind heckling or people making a nuisance of themselves. He argued that it reminded him of what he was there to do."

During the three-week campaign, John was driven around the constituency by Roger Juggins.

Roger had handed the reins of his Great Stukeley farm over to his son Stephen, who then broke his arm playing rugby a few days later and ended up joining the campaign team. Roger said:

"Some days there would be two meetings in the morning, then it was a quick lunch, two meetings in the afternoon, stop for a cup of tea and another two or three in the evening.

"We often used to joke that we became connoisseurs of cheap wine and bad cheese. The hardest thing was when the meeting broke up because everyone wanted to chat to John. I learned the knack of saying: 'Sorry John, but we're 10 minutes late already,' and whisking him away without offending anyone."

The spring of 1983 was the wettest on record in Huntingdon. Farmers in the area, who had lost much of their potato crop, were calling it disastrous.

There was severe flooding in St Neots and St Ives. The

new Hinchingbrooke Hospital was due to open a few weeks later and the rail service had improved only slightly.

During the campaign, David Steel, the leader of the Liberal Alliance Party, stopped off in Huntingdon to talk to voters. His Party was expecting to do well locally. The Liberal Alliance candidate for Huntingdon, Sheila Gatiss, came second and Labour candidate Mark Slater lost his deposit.

John was re-elected as MP for Huntingdon, with a 20,348 majority, almost identical to the 1979 figure, despite having 20,000 fewer electors. He said he had expected the Alliance Party to do well, but thought Mark Slater should not be blamed for the poor support for Labour, saying:

"I think Labour's national campaign was a shambles and their policies bore as much relation to the twentieth century as King Canute."

The Ecology Party candidate Tim Eiloart, who also lost his deposit, was delighted to have received 444 votes. He said he was especially pleased as most of the votes came from St Ives where he had managed to distribute 150 leaflets.

Sir Anthony Grant became the new MP for SW Cambs, taking 56 per cent of the vote.

Although John and Norma liked living in Hemingford Grey, they wanted a bigger house for their growing family. Eventually they bought a four-bedroomed house, called Finings, in Great Stukeley, just outside Huntingdon. It was Norma who discovered the house. She came across it on one of her many solo house-hunting trips and knew it would win favour with her husband. She said:

"He said it sounded perfect just from my description. I knew he wanted somewhere that would be a true family home, set in its own grounds and this fitted the bill perfectly. We had to take out a bridging loan, so we were stretched financially, but it was a decision we have never regretted."

THE PRIVATE MAJOR

The house, built in 1938, is not particularly grand, but it has just over two acres of land overlooking farmland, which was enough for John to fall in love with it the first time he saw it. He recalled:

"The grounds and the seclusion attracted me. And when we went to see it, we went through the main entrance up the gravel pathway and we went through a wonderful entrance with the lime trees on either side to the turning circle where the big cedar tree is, and before I got out of the car, before I had seen the whole of the garden, before I had seen the inside of the house, I just knew, from the atmosphere from the outside of the house, that it was the one I wanted. I remember thinking to myself that I don't have any idea what the inside is like and we might have to tear everything out, but this is what I want. I never had the slightest doubt. It was the second best impulse buy of my life, after Norma."

A few weeks before, the Majors had been "gazumped" out of a house on Riverside Park, St Neots, so to secure this place was important to them.

The rooms are not huge, but the conservatory, which was built on the back of the house a few years ago, is a refuge for John. A brick wall on one side of the hexagonal-shaped building is lined with bookcases. Most of the books are about cricket, and many of them were gifts, presents from well-wishers. Cane furniture and pot plants give the room a relaxed feel. Several pottery jugs and vases, a photograph of John and James dressed in dinner jackets, and John's cricketing memorabilia, add the personal touches.

A large bay window overlooks the garden and his pond, which was built in 1995. The Koi carp, which are always swimming near the surface, are so tame they can be fed by hand. A fountain in the middle of the water and a wooden garden bench on the patio next to the pond gives the whole setting a tranquil feel.

John loves to walk around the garden and look at his fruit trees and plants. The garden has provided a welcome retreat from the rigours of politics. It is here he has mulled

over decisions and taken time out to gather his thoughts.
He said:

"There have been moments, during some of the more difficult times,
when coming home to Huntingdon and looking round the garden to
see what's growing, preparing what you're actually going to do with
the garden and how you're going to remodel it, has been of great help.
There is a fascination about starting something or having it started and
seeing how it develops. I like to wander around and see how the
hedge is growing and how the pond is developing and what has
happened to the fruit trees we planted. Every weekend, I have a
statutory march around the garden and see how it's developing."

Lady Blatch recalls when she first saw the house:

"I can remember his real excitement when they bought the house.
We had been to a meeting one Saturday morning, before they moved
in, and he just took me round this empty house. The great thrill was,
this was a house in its own grounds, in a place that he loved and
close to everything . . . close to the town and people . . . never-the-
less very independent. It was the first time he had not had neighbours
cheek by jowl. He had lived in Brixton, which was very built up, so this
was special to him. He's as enthusiastic about the house and
Huntingdon today as when he first moved in. It made him feel good to
know he was providing well for his family and life was becoming more
settled. He had known times when his parents didn't have money,
anybody who's been in a family that struggled and who arrives at a
position where they have a relatively well-paid job and can afford a
mortgage and a house can feel well pleased with their efforts.
"He had genuinely done it himself, this was his own efforts, he had
worked extraordinarily hard and I think it gave him great pleasure."

Although Norma loved the house – it was perfect for a
growing family – she complained constantly about the
rabbits which came in from the fields at the back. Not being
familiar with country ways, she wasn't sure how to solve
the problem until Cyril Bridge popped round for tea one
day:

THE PRIVATE MAJOR

"I told Norma that I'd just been into town to buy an 4.10 air rifle. Her face lit up and she asked me if she could borrow it. She used to stick it out the kitchen window and take pot shots at the rabbits. I don't know if she actually managed to hit any rabbits, but it made her feel better anyway."

John was often asked to defend the Government's position on a particular subject at local meetings, which he enjoyed all the more if it was a controversial issue.

On one occasion he was addressing a Conservative political committee at the Brampton Hotel and opened the meeting by confirming; "I have not come here to apologise for the sinking of the Belgrano."

He told the assembled audience: "The Falklands had been invaded without provocation, British ships had been sunk and lives had been lost. The crew of the Belgrano were not there to get a suntan."

In her autumn reshuffle in 1984, Margaret Thatcher appointed John senior whip, giving him the formal title of Lord Commissioner of the Treasury.

The day of the announcement was his 14th wedding anniversary. John and Norma met on April 9, 1970, at Brixton Conservative Association. They both say it was love at first sight, the first thing John noticed was her big brown eyes.

Within three weeks they were engaged and married five months later at St Matthew's Church in Brixton. Shortly before the wedding, John' mother, who had been ill for some time, died, aged 65. His father Tom had died when he was 19.

John's workload increased with each new Government post, but the pressures really began in September, 1985, when he was promoted to the Department of Health and Social Security. It was here, as a junior minister under the direction of Norman Fowler, that he received his first taste of negative publicity. He said:

"The job of junior minister in what was then the combined

Department of Health and Social Security is one of the paper intensive jobs of Whitehall. I had a pretty large workload and for the first time I started bringing red boxes home and would spend the whole of the weekend working on boxes. So the family were pretty tolerant. It was a good thing we lived in such a friendly village and things had settled down so well."

Norma, without fuss and a great deal of complaint, was running their home, taking care of the children, supporting her husband in the constituency, and somehow had still found time to write a book.

Nine years of research went into her biography of opera soprano Joan Sutherland. The 110,000-word book described Dame Joan's professional career and was approved by the singer who wrote the introduction.

Most of the information has come from Norma, who compiled a catalogue of all the singer's performances.

The January of 1986 was extremely cold, and when the national media began running stories of old people dying of hypothermia, John, who was in charge of the system of paying heating support to the elderly and people on benefit, was put in the firing line. He said:

"For two or three days. I was the most hated man in England, largely on the basis of what the national Press had reported inaccurately rather than on the basis of anything I had done or was thinking of doing."

He managed to negotiate a £5 weekly increase and things blew over quite quickly, but the ferocity of the criticism took John by surprise. It was a feeling to which, in time, he would have to become accustomed.

HAPPY BIRTHDAY

THE Conservatives won all but two of the available seats at the local district council elections in the May of 1987. Huntingdonshire District Council was now made up of 44 Conservative, five Labour, two Alliance and two independent councillors. But in the run-up to the General Election, which had been called for June 11, not everyone in the constituency was happy with Conservative policies and decisions.

For instance, an announcement to increase the business rate by 33 per cent was met with condemnation by the business community, who were describing it as: "irresponsible." And, according to Huntingdon town councillors, the ring road had reached traffic saturation point and there were no signs of any improvement.

Despite these rumblings of discontent, John Major increased his majority to 27,044 after polling 40,530 votes at the 1987 Election. The victory gave him the largest Parliamentary majority in Huntingdonshire history.

The SDP/Liberal Alliance candidate Tony Nicholson was in second place, with 13,486 votes and Labour candidate David Brown, who was to be Hugh Seckleman's agent in the 1992 election, was third with 8,883 votes. Green Party candidate Barry Lavin doubled his 1983 vote to 874.

After Margaret Thatcher's post-election reshuffle, John was promoted to the Cabinet as Chief Secretary to the Treasury.

He has often said that it was the most difficult political post he has had, including that of Prime Minister.

The job involves negotiating Government expenditure with ministers, and John made it clear from the beginning that he was not going to be writing any 'blank cheques'.

His promotion caused some concern in Huntingdon. There were fears that he would not be able to devote as much time to the constituency. He was, after all, the first Huntingdon MP since Oliver Cromwell to make the Cabinet.

Roger Juggins felt it appropriate to issue a statement to the local Press and assure *Hunts Post* readers that John's new role would make not make any difference to the time he would have available to spend on constituency business.

In December, after the signing of the Super Power Treaty between America and the Soviet Union banning medium and short-range missiles, the peace campers at RAF Molesworth organised a party outside the base.

Local residents felt they had even more to celebrate as they watched the missiles and the peace campers leaving, although five stubborn protesters remained, camping in a lay-by for some time.

A study, carried out by the Standing Conference of East Anglian Local Authorities in May, 1988, showed that the Ouse Valley area was one of the fastest growing parts of the country. There was an average population increase of two per cent a year. The area's close proximity to Cambridge, the recent electrification of the railway line from Peterborough to London and the proposed A1/M1 link road, which was encouraging businesses to relocate to the area, were all thought to be responsible for the rapid rise in the population.

Such was the affection for John in the Huntingdon Association, when he had been Huntingdon's MP for 10 years, the members decided to have a party for him and Norma to mark the occasion.

Lady Blatch, who was organising the event, booked Elton Hall, a large country house surrounded by parkland in the village of Elton near Peterborough, and had 200 tickets printed. Once people started applying for tickets, it became clear that 200 would not be enough and it was upped to 300, then 400 and finally 500. The decision was made to stop at 500 and draw up a waiting list. Lady Blatch hired a marquee and the event was held in the grounds.

The guest speaker was Nigel Lawson, the then Chancellor of the Exchequer, who arrived by helicopter, landing in the grounds of the Sixteenth Century hall.

The marquee was lined with candelabra, and the guests wearing dinner jackets and ball gowns created an elegant setting on that balmy June evening. A cake had been made in the shape of a book and on one side was a potted biography of John's achievements to date. The cake was placed on a small table in front of the top table and the guests were urged to go to the front to look at it. Lady Blatch remembers:

"There were so many people there, that we were concerned that not everybody would see the cake. There was hardly a soul who came to that table that John didn't know by name and also the names of the wives, husbands and children and sometimes even the aunts and uncles. Nigel Lawson was genuinely gob-smacked. He actually said to me there was no way his constituency could have arranged a function like that. Frankly, I've always thought that Nigel Lawson thought the crowd pull was him, but it was quite clear that this was a John Major constituency function. All our functions are a bit like that. There would hardly be anyone he didn't know. That's the way he worked the constituency. He earned the support he received."

On Monday, July 24, 1989, Margaret Thatcher stunned the media and her Cabinet colleagues by promoting John to the post of Foreign Secretary.

The call from Downing Street came just after 4pm, around the same time that John, Norma and constituency agent Peter Brown, who was in Cornwall on holiday at the time, had resigned themselves to the fact that there was not going to be a promotion this time round.

Reshuffles are always a time for speculation, but no-one could possibly have guessed the outcome of this one in summer of 1989. One of the highest offices of state went to a man hardly recognised outside his own constituency. His predecessor, Sir Geoffrey Howe, was appointed deputy Prime Minister and leader of the House of Commons.

Douglas Hurd had been tipped for the post and wanted it desperately. John most definitely didn't want the job and knew Norma would want him to have it even less. To make matters worse, John hates flying and Norma suffers from travel sickness. John said:

> "It was a job I wasn't expecting to get, didn't especially want and for which my background had not especially prepared me. There was somebody else, in my judgement, who was patently better able to have the job than me and didn't get it. I grew to like the job very quickly, but it was emphatically not a job I sought and was a job Norma hoped I would never get. It meant a lot more travelling and a lot more gatherings and receptions and that sort of thing, which would inevitably involve Norma and we still had a young family. Elizabeth was coming up to her exams and James wasn't far behind. It was just a bad moment for a job like that."

Domestically, that short stint at the Foreign Office, was the most turbulent in the Major household. Part of the upheaval was the effect the new security, which appeared overnight, had on the family. By the time John returned to Finings that Thursday night, his home had become a fortress. There was a policeman with a machine gun standing at the gate, a perimeter fence had been erected and there was a caravan parked in the driveway which housed security men and their equipment.

The children had to be escorted to Kimbolton School, no longer allowed to walk about freely and queue for the school bus. The burden of their father's job was weighing heavily on their shoulders. John said:

> "I resented that security. It was a huge invasion into the private lives of Norma and the children. I could see it was necessary, but I resented it. There was the caravan sat by the side of the path with policemen in it. So, suddenly, this private home, which I had partly

valued for its immense charm, partly for its seclusion, suddenly had quite a lot of other visitors. Plus, of course, we place was, at times, pretty much under siege by members of the Press. I should say that, over the years, we have become used to the security and the people who are there because of it have become part of our extended family."

The only consolation for Norma was that the metal security fence would keep out the rabbits.

By the time the family had adjusted and become used to the security arrangements, everything had changed and John, who was only at the Foreign Office for three months, had moved on.

But during that 12 weeks, the foundations of bitterness and jealousy, which would resurface later when John was least expecting it, were laid. He said:

"Politics breeds its own antagonisms and it was obvious that some people thought I had been promoted far too fast. If I had been given the transport department or Northern Ireland, it would have been well received by my colleagues."

A survey in the *Economist* magazine, carried out just after the promotion was announced, showed that only two per cent of the population had heard of John Major.

His public image has often been poor, but the perception of him as grey and uninteresting is partly down to his own reluctance to push himself forward into the limelight. His refusal to court the media in the same way Margaret Thatcher did, was taken as a snub.

This, his honest approach and refusal to be become involved in any kind of spin doctoring, left him vulnerable and an easy target for the media to poke fun at.

'Does Mr Major have a valid passport?' inquired one newspaper after the announcement of his promotion to the Foreign Office. To which he replied later: "Contrary to what some sections of the media think, I have been beyond the white cliffs of Dover."

Although Huntingdon and his Great Stukeley home

became his refuge, John and Norma were never safe from prying eyes and camera lenses.

Most of those close to the family have at some stage been pestered for a piece of information, a photograph or insight into John and Norma's marriage. A loose word or a careless statement would be seen as treachery in the extended family of party and association members in Huntingdon.

The elaborate security at Finings offered protection, but there were occasions when even the Special Branch tactics could not prevent a persistent photographer from getting a picture.

The family have often watched photographers climb the trees, which surround the house, and tie themselves to the branches to get a shot. A row of strategically placed and fast-growing conifers were planted in front of the existing trees a few years ago to prevent any further intrusion.

The house is situated on a fairly sharp bend and on the opposite side of the road there is a built-up area of grass. It is a prime position to place a television camera or for someone to stand with a tele-photo lens. A photographer once camped there for days to snatch a photograph of John in his garden. Norma has never forgiven him – mainly because he was a local man.

In time, John learned the art of stifling a yawn and trying not to scratch at public events. And he always remembered rule number one; when the pressure is on, never stand under an exit sign!

But nothing could stop picture editors from using a photograph showing a particular expression and claiming it proved something else.

When he was first became Prime Minister in 1990, one national newspaper declared he had lost a stone in weight in his first few weeks and lost his voice because he was under so much stress.

Norma laughed and said: "He is tired and he's not getting a lot of sleep, but apart from that he's fighting fit."

THE PRIVATE MAJOR

Lady Blatch says:

"He wouldn't kowtow to some of the media, he would meet them and talk to them, but what he wouldn't do is play their game or enter into some kind of deal. John and Norma have been hurt by the lengths some of the paparazzi have gone to get pictures. On one occasion, during the 1990 leadership election, I had to go in the boot of a car to see John because he couldn't get out of his house. Anything that was high, they were in it or on it. Later it was the stories about the children that upset them most. The media followed Elizabeth around and ran stories about hers and James's first relationships. John posed willingly and happily for millions of pictures over the years – none of that he minded. It was the intrusive and personal nature of the reporting and when they slanted the story or tried to drag the children into the limelight simply because they were his children. He didn't see the point of that."

Roger Juggins believes:

"In the mid-80s, things built up and the media always seem to be on the prowl, and some politicians are easy targets. Eventually, we're not going to have anybody willing to stand as a leading politician. Someone who has been really successful in business and is in a position in their early forties to give ten or fifteen years to the country, will think twice. Fewer and fewer people will be willing to take the chance that an indiscretion or a schoolboy prank will be found out and splashed across the front pages of a newspaper. The Conservative Party has lost some really good people that we couldn't afford to lose."

Just as John was beginning to settle down at the Foreign Office, events made him change direction again. Nigel Lawson announced his resignation as Chancellor. His relationship with Mrs Thatcher had been fraught for some time. Finally, on October 26, 1989, he told the Prime Minister he was standing down.

Unlike Foreign Secretary, Chancellor of the Exchequer was a job John knew he could do well from the outset. His background in banking had prepared him well.

John has never minded hard work, but the workload was

such that he now found it necessary to put in around 18 hours a day, seven days a week. Food has always been fitted in around the more important tasks, but he will always make the time for a plate of fish and chips. He would often stop off at the Conservative club in Huntingdon and say: "I haven't eaten since breakfast, I'd love a plate of chips."

Norma describes her husband as having: "no interest in food." She said:

"He likes plain cooking, but then again, he likes chillis and spicy things like curries and casseroles. He's also very fond of traditional roasts. One of the stories which has gone around is that he likes peas, but he doesn't particularly; his favourite vegetable is broccoli and he's partial to parsnips, too. He doesn't have a sweet tooth at all, he doesn't go for desserts cakes or chocolate at all. Neither of us diet or go in for keep fit. We are lucky to be active and that keeps us fit enough."

BLUE IS THE COLOUR

T HE avalanche of condemnation over the Poll Tax – or
Community Charge to give it its formal title – was as
ferocious in Huntingdon as it was elsewhere in the
country.

John Major's attempt to quell protest in the constituency
by saying: "I do believe that once it is fully understood, it
will be seen to be a very much fairer system than the old
rating system," only fuelled local anger.

Throughout the spring of 1990, thousands of people, from
all sections of the community, appeared before Huntingdon
Magistrates' Court for refusing to pay Poll Tax.

An Anti-Poll Tax Union was set up, urging members to
delay payment for as long as possible. Liability Orders,
giving Huntingdonshire District Council power to seize
goods, deduct money from wages or send in bailiffs, were
issued to 1069 people at one hearing alone.

Angry crowds gathered outside the court house, in
Huntingdon Market Square, waving banners and chanting:
"We won't pay the Poll Tax."

Red paint had been daubed over the walls of the court and,
in an attempt to delay the proceedings, someone had
superglued the locks of the main doors. With more than
4000 summonses still waiting to be sent out, the district
council was struggling to cope with the rising number of
defaulters.

One protester went along to the cash office at Pathfinder
House, Huntingdon, to pay a month's Poll Tax with 2900
pennies. The cashier only just managed to suppress a smile
as she informed him she needed to count every penny

before she could issue a receipt.

In July, Ramsey man Hugh Seckleman announced his intention to stand against John at the next election. The 26-year-old Labour candidate wasted no time in launching his first attack, describing John as: "Margaret Thatcher's poodle."

He added: "Mrs Thatcher has brought him from obscurity to his present position to reward his unwavering devotion to her and her discredited policies."

As the new president of the Huntingdon branch of Mencap, one of Norma Major's first tasks was to launch a fund-raising appeal for a respite home in Peterborough. She organised a half marathon and fun run and agreed to take part in the half marathon, but made it clear she would only be walking the 13-mile course.

The appeal was going well. Events such as charity balls and horse races were bringing in thousands of pounds. In 1990, the charity received a boost when Alconbury Sports and Social Club decided to donate the money from its annual cricket match for her favourite charity.

John was asked to play, but had to decline because of a leg injury. He had broken his left leg in several places and damaged the knee cap in a car accident in Nigeria in 1967, while he was working for the Standard Chartered Bank, but he agreed to umpire and captain the Mencap team.

On this occasion John and Norma were in their element. The John Major XI played a Brian Close XI, giving John the chance to meet some of the sport's heroes while Norma got to spend time with her husband and raise money for Mencap.

Mrs Thatcher became more and more unpopular as 1990 progressed into the autumn. The widespread Poll Tax riots, her apparent indecision over European issues and the worsening economy were seriously undermining her authority.

She could have limped on with public opinion against her, but when Sir Geoffrey Howe stood down as deputy leader and savaged her in his resignation speech, many of her colleagues thought she was doomed.

The rumour machine swung into action and former minister Michael Heseltine, amid growing media speculation, announced his decision to stand against her, forcing a leadership election in which Conservative MPs at Westminster could vote.

The result of the first ballot on November 20 shocked everyone. Mr Heseltine gained 152 votes to Mrs Thatcher's 204. She needed to win more than half the votes in the first ballot to be safe.

In Huntingdon, constituency agent Peter Brown was insisting that John would not be putting his name forward as a candidate and intended to second Mrs Thatcher in the second ballot on November 27. But the following morning, Mrs Thatcher told her Cabinet she had decided to resign. The Iron Lady, who had served 11 years as Prime Minister and 15 as leader of the Conservative Party, finally let her guard down. She started to cry as she read from her prepared statement and handed it to someone else to finish reading for her.

John was not around to witness the painful events of that Wednesday morning. He had undergone an operation to remove a painful wisdom tooth and was recovering at home. So it was Norma who was left to answer the phone at Finings, which seemed to ring every five minutes, and relay messages to John from colleagues and friends, most of them urging him to put his name forward and stand in the leadership election. She said:

"It was a mesmerising few days, totally exciting. There was so much going on, so much talking and planning. About 24 hours before the day of the election was really a high note, because we knew he would win. I suppose at the time, I did not know what was to come, but then you never really consider everything you should in life. My view was then, and it is now, that if that's what John wants to do and he's sure it is right, then that is what you do."

THE PRIVATE MAJOR

As he contemplated his political future at home, well away from the political machinations at Westminster, John was wrestling with his conscience. He wasn't sure if he had enough experience; he had only been Chancellor for 13 months, and didn't want to appear disloyal to Mrs Thatcher. Next to Mr Heseltine and Douglas Hurd, who had also announced his decision to stand in the leadership election, he was the rank outsider. He said:

"Undoubtedly, it would have been better if I'd had more time in the Cabinet. I had undergone a crash course in foreign affairs and at the Treasury. It would have been better from my point of view if I'd been able to spend a couple of years in the Foreign Office and a couple of years at the Treasury before becoming Prime Minister. It would probably have helped if I'd had a middle ranking job. I could have done with my own ministry as well, but in politics if you're offered a job, you say 'yes' or you say 'no'. You don't bargain with Prime Ministers. I did query with Mrs Thatcher whether it was wise to make me Foreign Secretary, but it was the end of the day and she had held it back. It was too late to change it and she had no intention of changing it. So you either say 'no', which is running away from challenge or you do it, you don't argue with Prime Ministers – not just Margaret Thatcher, any Prime Minister."

The only person he talked everything through with was Norma. Although she had reservations – like concerns about the affect it would have on family life – she decided that if it was going to happen one day anyway it may as well be now. She said:

"Many people misunderstood what I said at the time. Of course I totally supported my husband's decision, I was fully behind him. But James was still at school then and needed me back at home in Huntingdon. When I said the job wouldn't make any difference, I meant it, because John had been spending the week in London and then returning to Huntingdon for the weekend and that continued; there was no change to that routine. But some people thought I didn't want to have anything to do with my husband's work. Nothing could have been further from the truth. But the point was that, initially, there

49

THE PRIVATE MAJOR

was no infrastructure for my role, so until there was we continued as we had done."

But John still felt uncomfortable about the events leading up to Mrs Thatcher's demise and knew any successor was bound to be blamed for playing a part in her downfall:

"I don't think it was so much personal as politics became later, it was more about policy. It was more about the Poll Tax and European policy. I thought it was pretty appalling what some people chose to do at that time. I was still in my first year as Chancellor and was pretty wrapped up in my own job. One thing people have never recognised over the past few years, particularly before I became Prime Minister, is that I was always on a learning curve. I was never in any job long enough to see the cycle round twice. To an extent, I was so wrapped up with what went on at the Treasury that I didn't absorb the House of Commons atmosphere as much as many others. The legacy of those events have cast a long shadow throughout the last seven years for a raft of complex reasons. It would have been infinitely preferable, from my point of view, and from everybody else's, if the matter hadn't gone as it did. It would have been difficult not to stand, because of the pressure on me from quite a large part of the Party, but it would not have broken my heart if I hadn't won."

Roger Juggins, like most of the association members in Huntingdon, felt the leadership issue had come too soon. It would have been better if John had served three or four more years in the Cabinet. He said:

"In politics you either grab it when it's there or lose it. He would have liked longer as Chancellor, but things moved on so quickly."

Lady Blatch said:

"A lot of us were deeply upset at the demise of Margaret Thatcher — the callousness and speed with which it happened. But politics is politics and once she'd gone, she'd gone. People believed she would not have won the next General Election and she had come to a point where her contact with people was less than it should have been.

50

THE PRIVATE MAJOR

Those of us who know John Major, and I will believe it until I go to my grave, know that he was somebody who would never have wanted to become Prime Minister in that way. It just wasn't the way he hoped it would happen. The job he always aspired to was Chancellor of the Exchequer. We are an incredible Party – overnight we ditch Margaret Thatcher, the next thing we know we have a new Prime Minister."

John based his leadership campaign on what he termed the 'classless society'. It was misunderstood by some, but he believed strongly that if people wanted to better themselves, their efforts should not be thwarted by artificial barriers, such as prejudice or a poor background. If somebody had talent and had worked hard, the first rung of the ladder should be available to them. It was not about levelling down and he wasn't hostile to the upper classes because of his own background. He saw a value in everybody.

He was relaxed throughout the leadership campaign and says he felt no antagonism towards the other candidates. He was fairly certain that whoever won, his job at the Treasury would be secure.

As the political debate and in-depth analysis about his chances were being thrashed out at the highest levels, back in his constituency some people were more than confident of his success.

Paddy Swallow, landlord of the Three Horseshoes pub in Great Stukeley concocted the *Major Upset* – a cocktail which he managed to get as near to Conservative blue as possible. Although he would not reveal all the ingredients, he did say it contained whisky and rum. The cocktail, selling for £2 a glass, was proving popular with his regulars.

"I've been waiting for Mr Major to come in and try it, but I expect he's been a bit busy," joked Mr Swallow.

John decided to stay over at Number 11, official residence of the Chancellor, during the weekend before the leadership election because there was so much work to do. He did, however, find the time to put in a call to Chelsea

THE PRIVATE MAJOR

Football Club to wish his team luck in their match with Manchester United on the Sunday. The Blues won 3-2. Meanwhile at Huntingdon Races, on the day of the contest, two horses were withdrawn at the last minute. The first was the legendary Desert Orchid and the second was a horse called Major Effort.

Media interest grew to new levels. Reporters waiting outside Finings were counting the cost of their doorstep encampment when a car came off the road outside the house, and hit four parked vehicles and a television camera belonging to the BBC's *Look East* team.

Before Norma could travel to London on the Monday night, she had to make sure everything at Finings was going to run smoothly in her absence. So it was arranged for her mother Dee to stay at the house. On the Tuesday morning, the day of the election, Norma packed a few of John's favourite meals and snacks and drove to the capital.

On the morning of November 27, John made his way to Committee Room 12 at Westminster to cast his vote and then spent the rest of the day at Number 11. He slept from 2.30pm until 6pm and awoke refreshed. That evening, the flat, which Norma had tried to make homely during the past year by bringing personal possessions from the Great Stukeley house, was crammed with people.

The result came through at 6.20pm; Michael Heseltine received 131 votes, Douglas Hurd 56 and John Major 185. It wasn't enough for anyone to win outright, but minutes later, Mr Heseltine announced his decision to withdraw from the contest. This was closely followed by Mr Hurd's announcement to do the same.

Just minutes after the result was announced, John spoke to *The Hunts Post*, saying: "I hope the people of Huntingdon will be pleased. I still regard myself primarily as the MP for Huntingdon and will continue to maintain the family home in Great Stukeley." He said Mrs Thatcher had been "very supportive" and had given him a hug when she heard the news.

THE PRIVATE MAJOR

Now John really was big news, something which wasn't lost on *Cambridge Evening News* reporter Julian Makey, a former chief reporter of *The Hunts Post*. Julian, who had known John ever since his arrival in Huntingdon — he had covered the last 18 months of Lord Renton's tenure — left the St Ives district office of his regional daily newspaper, went to London to cover the story and grabbed his biggest "scoop" – the first face-to-face newspaper interview with the new Premier. He recalled:

"We had been trying to get hold of him for some time, without success, not because he didn't want to talk to us, but because there was so much going on I doubt if he even got the messages. So I went down to London on the Saturday before the leadership contest, when he held a press conference and managed to have a brief word with him to tell him we really wanted an interview. He said he would do the best he could.

"On the day of the leadership contest, I was at the House of Commons and photographer Roger Adams was in the scrum at Downing Street. The first result wasn't conclusive, so I'd resigned myself to going back with nothing. Then news came through that the other candidates had withdrawn. A few minutes later, one of the press officers, Gus O'Donnell, I think, came over and said: 'Is there anyone here from the *Cambridge Evening News*?' Me and Roger were invited into Number 11. There were quite a few people there, including Norma, so I had a chat with her. She said she was pleased, but was still coming to terms with her husband being Prime Minister. It turned out George Bush had rung to wish John all the best from Airforce One, which was why he wasn't there. Anyway, while I was still talking to Norma, he just put his head around the door and gave us that mild smile. He looked totally unexcited. It looked like he'd just won a small raffle prize at a village fete. We did the interview and he was anxious to make the point that Huntingdon was still home and it wouldn't make any difference to his commitment to the constituency. I think he wanted to be fair to the constituency and wanted people here to get a fair crack of the whip; he didn't want the local newspapers to be left behind."

Julian has followed John's career from the constituency.

THE PRIVATE MAJOR

Although he has seen many changes, he claims to have only seen him angry once – when media intrusion into James' private life had particularly upset Norma – and says his MP is always confident and in charge of any situation which confronts him. He said:

"I have always found him to be an honest, genuine and likeable man with a good sense of humour, but I think the pressures of being Prime Minister changed that, or he felt he had to pull back from being like that at times. He's different to the *Spitting Image* puppet, which didn't help — I think that sort of thing made him more cautious in his dealings with the media. He is a man who always seems to be in control, which might surprise people who don't know him. A lot of what he does wasn't of interest to the nationals, so most people didn't have any idea of what he was really like. For instance, he would send handwritten notes to people who had suffered a death in the family or something. He was an extremely good constituency MP. He always seemed to deal with smaller groups better than the huge setpiece things he had to get involved with as Prime Minister. Loads of times you would talk to people coming out of those events and they'd say: 'I never knew he was like that.' I think he fitted the constituency very well – we're a pretty unexcitable lot here and we don't like flash people."

At 47, he was the youngest Prime Minister of the Twentieth Century. He had only been in the Cabinet for three years and a Member of Parliament for 11.

Norma joined him on the steps of Number 10 to face a sea of flashbulbs and microphones. As John made a speech thanking his supporters, contingency plans to once again increase the security at Finings in order to protect the new Prime Minister were speedily put into place.

In Huntingdon, the usually subdued halls of The Views were bursting with excitement. Party members, television crews and newspaper reporters were jostling for space.

The hushed silence as the result was announced from a television screen on the wall had now erupted into rapturous applause and excitement. The initial disappointment on hearing that John had missed out by two votes and the issue would go to a second ballot was replaced by screams of delight and cheers when Mr Heseltine and Mr Hurd withdrew from the contest.

Bottles of Champagne, which had been kept out of the way until the result was known, were brought out and cracked opened.

When 15-year-old James Major, who was sitting next to his grandmother, was asked by one reporter how he felt about his father's success, he said: "I am very excited and extremely pleased for him, although I suppose it will mean I will see even less of him. I do not know much about his life in politics, but as far as I'm concerned he is the best dad I could have."

Peter Brown, John's agent, said he was "numb with emotion." District councillor Pree Newbon quipped: "He will be the first Prime Minister with a sense of humour." Cyril Bridge was claiming to have predicted the event 10 years earlier. Gary Rule, chairman of Huntingdon Young Conservatives, added: "The Conservative Party has got to look for the young vote and what better way to do it than having a young leader to look up to."

During all the excitement of the previous few days and her concern for John, who was still in pain from his tooth, Norma had hardly had a moment to herself and was exhausted. In her haste to join her husband on arguably the most important occasion of his career so far, she had not packed enough clothes.

The following day they had to go to Buckingham Palace where John would receive the official seal of office from the Queen. Norma had no choice, but to wear the suit she had worn the night before as she stood on the steps of Number 10. It was a blue *Jacques Vert* suit, which John liked and one which she felt comfortable wearing. She thought nobody would notice her outfit as there were far more important things to comment upon.

As the official Daimler made its way down The Mall, John and Norma were both deep in thought, struggling to take in the events of the previous night. It never occurred to either of them that Norma's outfit would warrant so much media attention the next day. She was savaged by the fashion writers and columnists who couldn't understand why she had not made more effort for her husband. Why couldn't she have worn a different outfit to the Palace, the headlines demanded. Roger Juggins says:

"Anyone else would have walked down the nearest High Street and bought something else to wear, but that would not have entered Norma's head. She said afterwards, it just never occurred to her, there was too much else to think about. She hates wasting money. When they first started flying around the world, all the expense made her uncomfortable, but she learned to live with it because she had to."

In the following few days, several of John and Norma's friends from the constituency telephoned to offer their congratulations. When Lady Blatch rang and John answered, she addressed him as 'sir'. He told her: "Emily, you are a dear friend and I have known you a long time. Please continue to call me John."

Long before the leadership election, a Huntingdon Conservative Club dinner had been planned for November 30 at The Views. They were grand affairs, held each year. The current leader of the Party was always invited to this black tie event. As it was only three days after the election, most people assumed that John and possibly Norma as well wouldn't be able to make it.

But they didn't disappoint, and as they walked through the door there was euphoria, said Roger Juggins. "We were more than flattered. We would have understood it if he hadn't have made it."

After the dinner, John stood up to make a speech. He allowed himself a wry smile before saying: "I hope you have noticed that Norma has the blue suit on."

The room erupted with laughter. Among friends he felt comfortable making a joke about something which, at the time, had caused him and Norma a great deal of pain and anguish.

Like coming home at the end of a long, hard day, making light of a difficult situation helped to relieve the pressure. Here in Huntingdon, John and Norma were understood and appreciated, but outside the cocoon of the constituency, life would never be the same again.

TEAM CAPTAIN

A FEW days after John Major had become Prime Minister, he sat in his chair in the Cabinet room at Number 10 Downing Street and made a list. He wrote down the words: *inflation, unemployment, Northern Ireland* and *Europe*. These were the issues he believed would dominate the next five years and he made it his personal mandate to bring about solutions. He said:

"I always loathed inflation. I thought no Government had tackled inflation properly since the early 1950s. It had wrecked our economy time and time again. I thought someone at some stage was going to have to see through all the unpleasant things that need to be done to rid our economy of endemic inflation. I always thought it was intolerable that Northern Ireland was pushed on the back-burner of British politics, with all the carnage that had gone on there. If that had gone on in Huntingdonshire, we would never have accepted it, so why should we accept it in Ireland? You need to know what you would most wish to do and making that list clarified my mind. The criticism that most people have made in recent years is that we didn't know what we were doing or where we were going. Very possibly we were bad at explaining it in the torrid political atmosphere."

One of John's first visitors to 10 Downing Street the day after the leadership election was Michael Heseltine. The two men posed for photographs on the steps outside and then John spent the afternoon appointing his first Cabinet.

John and Norma could have spent that first and every other weekend at Chequers, the Prime Minister's Buckinghamshire retreat, but chose instead to return to Huntingdon. Not that Norma saw much of her husband, for he spent most of the weekend working on despatch boxes and Government papers.

On the Saturday night, John and Norma surprised members of the Glatton and Conington branch of the Conservative Association by popping in for Christmas dinner at the village hall. The visit was unplanned – they wanted to thank people for their support. Later the same evening, he and Norma attended a constituency meeting in Bluntisham.

On the Sunday, John, Norma and Elizabeth posed for photographs in the garden at Finings, but John made it clear he would not be giving interviews – except to his local paper. He told *The Hunts Post* he was confident that he would still be able to lead a normal life with his family:

"I have never been particularly publicity hungry, but I shall learn to live with it without a great deal of difficulty."

But a year later he admitted:

"I do not own my own time any more and nor does Norma. I can't go out and do my shopping and I miss my privacy."

When the new Prime Minister was asked if he thought he would have any difficulty commanding respect from his more experienced Cabinet colleagues, he said:

"I don't believe so. I think they will judge me by what I do and indeed a large number of them supported me in the election contest, or I could not have won."

The cost, in terms of finance and manpower, of providing round-the-clock security for the new Prime Minister and his family in Huntingdon was weighing heavily on Cambridgeshire Constabulary. Assistant Chief Constable David Winser said forward planning in recent weeks had prepared them for the event, but responsibility for the family while they were in Huntingdon was causing some concern. Top-level discussions with the Home Office were planned to sort out more money.

The return of the dogs, alarms and panic buttons at Finings filled Norma with dread. When she and John arrived home that first weekend after the election, the caravan, which housed Special Branch officers and their equipment for the duration of John's stint at the Foreign Office, had been replaced by a permanent building in the corner of the driveway.

She knew it was all necessary. In June, John had been due to speak at a political lunch at the Carlton Club in St James' Street in London; 40 hours before his talk, an IRA bomb ripped the building apart. Only a busy day in the Commons prevented more MPs, who would usually have been lunching at the club, from being hurt.

Even taking all that into consideration, deep down she couldn't help feeling her orderly life had been turned inside out and upside down.

All around Huntingdon there was a feeling of great excitement about John becoming Prime Minister, but it was also tinged with a degree of sadness for some. The security arrangements at Finings meant friends could no longer pop in for a cup of tea, and many people had to face the fact that they wouldn't see John and Norma quite so often.

John loves Indian food and often used to pop into the New Delhi restaurant in Ermine Street in Huntingdon on a weekday evening with Norma. He usually chose his favourite chicken tikka masala which would be washed down with a glass of wine or beer. Norma preferred a milder dish, such as lamb rogan josh with a glass of mineral water. Manager Ullah Malik said at the time:

"Mr Major has been coming here ever since we opened seven years ago. He is a very good customer and very friendly. We just hope he gets chance to call in soon with his wife so we can congratulate him personally."

In fact, restaurant staff were so delighted to hear John had become Prime Minister, they placed a congratulatory advert in the *London Evening Standard.*

John's ascendancy had been so swift that there was no time to celebrate and hardly enough time for him to prepare himself for the tough tasks ahead.

By late 1990 war clouds were gathering. Iraqi leader Saddam Hussein's invasion of Kuwait on August 2, 1990, sparked the beginning of the Persian Gulf War. Huntingdonshire became caught up in the whirlwind of military and diplomatic activity.

Early reports revealed that two local men, Keith Greenwood, from St Ives, and Ray Washer, from Earith, had been captured and were part of Saddam's "human shield" of prisoners.

Although intervention by Sir Edward Heath secured their release in time for Christmas, Britain and its coalition allies were on the road to war with Iraq.

Hostilities began in January, 1991. A-10 pilots from RAF Alconbury based in the Gulf flew search and rescue missions to pick up crewmen shot down behind Iraqi lines. Support Command at RAF Brampton co-ordinated the provision of supplies to all RAF aircraft involved in the conflict.

The Gulf War was just one of the many pressures facing John during that first week in office. He said:

"I was plunged straight into work. You're elected one night, the next day you see the Queen and then there's the Cabinet reshuffle and you're in to Prime Minister's questions and the daily routine. What I inherited wasn't the greatest political inheritance of all time. The Party was desperately split over the Community Charge and it was clear it had to be abolished and replaced. The disputes about Europe were apparent; we were heading into a recession, interest rates were at 15 per cent and unemployment was going through the roof and we were about to embark on the Gulf War. That isn't the ideal scenario to inherit 18 months before the latest possible date for a General Election. There was a very real chance that I would be Prime Minister for a very brief time and that we would lose the next election."

THE PRIVATE MAJOR

As John grappled with the politics of the day, the media had a field day with his upbringing and personal appearance. The most important question of the day it seemed was not: 'How was he going to bring the Gulf War to a conclusion?' but: 'Did the new Prime Minister tuck his shirt into his underpants?'

Sir Anthony Grant, MP for South-West Cambridgeshire, hit back. He said:

"The chief quality required in a Prime Minister is not looks, not so-called charisma and not even oratory. It's judgement – judgement of issues and judgement of individuals. Mrs Thatcher was a great judge of issues, but John will be a better judge of individuals. He will be more of a team captain than a solo performer. His first Cabinet is thoroughly sensible. The decision to give Michael Heseltine the Poll Tax portfolio is shrewd, so too is his decision not to include a woman in the Cabinet, just because she is a woman. The statutory woman in the Cabinet concept is patronising and insulting to the female sex. Intelligent women want to be judged solely on their merits – not their sex. The outcry from a few silly women is wholly unjustified. It is as daft as complaining that there are too many or too few Etonians or redheads or bald heads."

John's relatively humble background, colourful early family life and lack of academic qualifications had journalists champing at the bit for more details.

In the 1920s, John's father Tom was an entertainer and skilled acrobat. He performed in a duo with a dancer called Gwen, who later became his second wife. John, the youngest of three children, spent his early years in the London suburb of Worcester Park where the family ran a business making garden gnomes. When he was 12, the business went bankrupt and the family moved to a two-bedroomed terraced house in Brixton.

After leaving Rutlish School in Merton, with a handful of O-Levels, he found work at insurance brokers Price Forbes, then went gnome-making for David's Rural Industries and as an electricity board clerk. He was unemployed for a while before joining the Standard Chartered Bank in 1966. These details now became of Press and public interest.

Although John and Norma had prepared themselves for this onslaught of interest in their private lives, they say the lack of privacy and intrusion became merciless over the years. He said:

"It doesn't only affect you, it affects your family as well. In Huntingdon, I came home and closed the door and people were very protective and supportive, but beyond that it wasn't true. As a public figure, I expected invasions of privacy and haven't been disappointed. Norma is quite reconciled to that and metaphorically our shoulders are broad. We put ourselves in the public eye and don't squeal about the publicity, but I don't think the same things applies to the children. They have been subjected to publicity which Norma and I think was intrusive and unnecessary."

In January, 1991, opinion polls made John the most popular Prime Minister since Winston Churchill, and the swift conclusion of the Gulf War boosted his prestige.

But, by March, the same polls showed Labour had overtaken the Conservatives. And, in May, the Conservatives lost more than 1000 seats in the local elections. When British Airways cut off donations to the Party in July, things began to look bleak for the Prime Minister.

John Bridge, the current chairman of the Conservative Association in Huntingdon, said:

"Bernard Ingham [*former Chief Press Secretary to Mrs Thatcher*] told me, that the biggest problem the Conservatives had after Margaret Thatcher went was keeping the Party together. He felt there was so much turbulence, that John was the only person who had the character and ability to do it. I don't think people realised what it took in the run-up to the 1992 election, the juggling involved to keep the wheels on the road and trying to drive through his economic policy. He was focused on what he needed to do, but it's my view that he put a few noses out of joint. He didn't believe in the hierarchical situation. In

THE PRIVATE MAJOR

John they had a Prime Minister who didn't concur with that view."

When John became Prime Minister, life in the constituency became fraught for a while.

Staff at the Conservative Association in Stukeley Road , Huntingdon, found it much more difficult to juggle his diary. There were so many demands on his time and every request had to be cleared with Downing Street. Even fairly low-key visits to local schools and factories meant tight security, a news blackout until the morning of the visit and the sniffer dogs had to search the building before John could set foot in the place.

Peter Brown found his responsibilities multiplied by the success of the man he simply calls: "The Boss." He said:

"Foreign Secretary is the third most important job in the Cabinet, so we suddenly had to devise a diary, a programme for him which took into account security arrangements. That was less so with the job of Chancellor, in fact security was downgraded then. But when he became Prime Minister, it was tighter than ever, although I was prepared for it. After he became Foreign Secretary, it was clear that some day the job might be his. He always wanted to play a full part in the constituency and show people he was still putting Huntingdon people first. Fortunately, he had built up this tremendous rapport with the constituency, so people understood that we had to try and fit engagements into an already-full diary. We had one constituency day a month and it was a really full day — he loves visiting places and talking to people. Gina Hearn, his Downing Street secretary, did a marvellous job in balancing all his engagements. I don't think anybody could say he neglected the constituency. Whenever he was around, so were the Press and television cameras. The bulk of my work was dealing with those demands."

Norma's role in the constituency became much more important after John became Prime Minister. Her commitment was never more apparent than on February 21, 1991. She had already heard the news on television that the IRA had launched a mortar bomb through the window of the Cabinet room at Number 10. Although nobody was

64

Time to relax . . . sharing a glass of port and lemon with 101-year-old Conservative voter Matilda Barlow on polling day, 1997 . . .

. . . and enjoying a cup of tea in April, 1997.
Picture: STEPHEN DANIELS

Hit for six – John Major the cricket umpire, a role he clearly relishes.

Norma Major enjoys some indoor cricket at the Hunts
Sports Centre . . .

. . . and gets
some useful
tips on taking
guard from
her husband
in 1995.

Public events don't always go smoothly, as this sequence
of pictures from March, 1983, show. John Major prepares
to launch a boat by smashing a bottle of champagne
against the side in the traditional manner, but as we can
see it's not as easy as it looks . . .

Announcement of election results in Huntingdon Market Square, June 16, 1983.

Major supporters have plenty of reason to jump for joy in 1983.

Lord David Renton, Tory grandee Lord Hailsham and John Major pictured in 1983.

Baroness Janet Young, centre, Jo Johnston and Roger Juggins with John and Norma Major in 1982.

Lord Renton pictured in 1979 and the late Lady Renton in a picture from 1969.

John Major and Lord Renton with a bust of the former Huntingdon MP in 1995.

Eric Forth, John Patten, Emily Blatch and Nigel Forman
while ministers at the Department of Education.

Father and son –
Cyril Bridge, left,
and John Bridge,
above.

Roger Juggins, Great Stukeley farmer and former chairman of Huntingdon Conservative Club.

Connie Jeffrey, *The Hunts Post's* Great Stukeley correspondent and a fierce critic of John Major.

Norma Major at the St Neots raft race.

John Major and his Grafham Water Lions namesake.

A meeting with constituents during his early days as MP in October, 1979.

With opposing candidates Sheila Gatiss, Mark Slater and Tim Eiloart at the June, 1983 election.

Signing a football for children in the constituency.

A face in a sea of children in 1996.

On the election trail.

April 16, 1992, with election veteran Screaming
Lord Sutch at the election count.

Norma at a book signing session of her Dame Joan
Sutherland biography, handing over a copy
to Pat Sawyer, in May, 1987.

At a cheque handover for Mencap in July, 1992, with
proceeds from the annual cricket match.

A supportive glance from the sidelines.

Picture: MMP CAMBRIDGE

Norma at a cricket match.

John Major's father Abraham Thomas, left, during his circus ring days.

SOMETIMES IT'S EASIER TO CHOOSE THE DRINKS THAN THE CABINET.

ARE YOU READY FOR A RUDDLES? (RUDDLES COUNTY)

The Ruddles brewing firm capitalise on John Major's fame in this advertisement.

On a visit to Great Staughton in the constituency, July, 1995.

Kimbolton School, where both Major children were educated.

The exterior of the Major family home at Great Stukeley.

Relaxing at home in the garden.

At home in an English country garden . . .

With election crowds in the spring of 1997.

Facing the demands of the media pack.

A losing
battle –
putting a
brave face
on it in
1997.

Looking back . . . John Major

hurt, it was obvious there had been a lapse in the tight security surrounding the Prime Minister. As John told the war cabinet members "I think we had better start again somewhere else," Norma prepared to start the charity pancake race in Huntingdon High Street. She said:

"I was on the telephone to the Downing Street secretary and there was this terrific noise in the background. The phone went dead. When they got back to me they said there had been a bomb."

She said after the race that she intended to cook James and Elizabeth pancakes for their tea that night and told onlookers that John really loved pancakes with lots of fresh lemon and sugar on top.

In May, John received a letter from John Major. At first, his staff thought it must be a publicity stunt, until they made some checks and found out there was actually a man called John Major living in the constituency. The less-famous Mr Major, who was president of the Huntingdon and Grafham Water Lions Club, a philanthropic charity organisation, wrote to the Prime Minister to ask him to start a sponsored walk around the shoreline of Grafham Water, a distance of 10 miles. He said:

"I suppose it was a bit of a cheeky letter, because I wrote: 'I've been receiving your post and taking your phone calls, now it's time you did something for me.' That bit was true and I was amazed that it happened. I moved to Perry (a small village on the edge of Grafham Water) from Wandsworth after the other John Major. In the London phone directory there were only about 20 Majors listed, so it's not a common surname. Soon after I arrived, there were stacks of post which I had to re-direct and numerous phone calls from all over the place in all sorts of languages; there are some real cranks about, I can tell you. I was amazed people thought the Prime Minister's telephone number would be listed; the calls only stopped when I went ex-directory. Anyway, he saw the funny side of the situation and agreed to start the event, which by his presence attracted national media and television interest. I was impressed, as was everyone else there. He was very warm, cheerful and down-to-earth and seemed to relate to everyone. He did a speech, which was very, very well received – I've videoed it – and he went around encouraging the walkers and treating everyone in such an warm-hearted way. Despite us both being active in the community, I've not met him since."

Having the Prime Minister or his wife agree to attend a fund-raising event will guarantee the crowds and inevitably raise a hefty sum of money at the end of the day. The annual Mencap cricket match at Alconbury has raised about £25,000 for the charity since 1990, when John agreed to umpire and captain a team.

But in the summer of 1991, Special Branch were unhappy about using John's name to publicise the event, because of the security risk, so the team was renamed the Norma Major Mencap XI. The committee had always managed to attract a sprinkling of stars, but this year, with the newly-elected Prime Minister in attendance, entertainers and cricketers were falling over themselves for a place in Norma's team.

The Alconbury Sports and Social Club committee had spent six months organising sponsors, guests, umpires, catering, advertising and mobile toilets. Providing food and entertainment for 200 people was no mean feat.

Players, including Gary Lineker, Bill Wyman, Gary Mason and Dr Hilary Jones started to arrive around midday, closely followed by hundreds of people. It was a security nightmare.

The committee had seriously underestimated the number of spectators attracted to the event, and there were about 3000 people milling around, several of them clambering to get into the changing rooms for an autograph. The plan for John and Norma's arrival would have to be changed. Instead of the official Daimler entering the main car park, it would use a back lane and the Majors would be directed down a footpath. The welcoming party of a local doctor, the head of British Gas and his wife, who was presenting a bouquet, and John and Norma were all ushered past the mobile toilets, over the guy-ropes and through the back of the beer tent to relative safety.

After David Essex phoned and said: "How the hell do I get to this place . . . Alconbury?" most people settled down to watch the cricket.

In September 1991, John ruled out a November election and immersed himself in the Maastricht Treaty on further European Union integration, which he claims was one of the most stressful times of his premiership. The treaty was concluded in the Dutch town with opt-outs for the UK before the end of the year, but was to undergo a traumatic passage through Parliament the following year. He said:

"Negotiating Maastricht was not too difficult, what was was seeing it through the House of Commons. I had these perpetual battles against people in my own Party who had agreed to what I should negotiate, cheered when I had negotiated it and now wished to change their minds. The point about this was, I had given my word in an international negotiation, after having got the consent of Parliament and now, having given my word, the British Government's word, some members of Parliament wished to break that word after we had done a deal and concessions had been made to it. It never occurred to me for a single second to break my word, the British Government's word."

On March 2, 1992, the General Election was announced for April 9, the anniversary of the day John and Norma met.

It was an election that John and the Conservatives were predicted, by most in the media and the bulk of opinion polls, to lose.

Many people now believe it was only John's hard work and personal approach that gave the Conservatives their surprise victory, in spite of the efforts of a few in the Party.

Lady Blatch says:

"There were some people who were deeply wounded by Mrs Thatcher going. This intellectual set had it in their minds that their favourite politician of all time had been deposed and here was this upstart, this man from Brixton, with no education who had never been to university with his stupid soapbox taking her place. The grieving

THE PRIVATE MAJOR

rippled on and the animosity began to build up. It was compounded because that group of people wanted us to lose the 1992 election – it would have put everything into place for them. Had we lost the 1992 election they could have said: 'Mrs Thatcher would have won it, John Major lost us the election, the Party will never be the same without her'.

It wasn't just that we won the election, when the historians look back they will see that he personally was responsible for winning it. He got out his soapbox, stood up in the highways and market squares up and down the country and caught the imagination of the people. The wound just went deeper and deeper and the next best thing to us not winning the election was to see him fail. A few people in pretty influential places set out to destroy him."

AGAINST ALL ODDS

J OHN Major refused to believe the opinion polls of the Spring of 1992. The nature of his campaigning meant he felt he was in a better position to gauge public opinion. His gut instinct convinced him the Conservative Party would win the election. He said:

"I was going round the country getting an extraordinary friendly reception and I didn't believe I'd got into Downing Street to be tossed out 18 months later. I thought all the way through the election that the opinion polls had read it wrongly, they had over-stated the Labour vote and under-stated the Conservative vote. There were some bad nights. One night in particular, I had flown back from the north and all the opinion polls had us at between seven and nine per cent behind, with about nine days to go. The Sunday before the election, when every newspaper had written us off and were preparing for a Neil Kinnock Government . . . that was a pretty bad day as well."

All Prime Ministers' constituencies over the years have become a magnet for fringe candidates seeking publicity. None fitted this bill better than Screaming Lord Sutch, who stood against John at the 1992 election. Lord Sutch, founder of the Official Monster Raving Loony Party, was the most experienced of all the Huntingdon candidates. He had fought more elections than all his opponents put together and lost his deposit more times as well. The 51-year-old former pop star, from Notting Hill in London, launched his campaign with the slogan: "Vote For Insanity, You Know It Makes Sense."

John had initially decided on a new style of political campaigning for this election.

69

THE PRIVATE MAJOR

He went around village halls with his shirt sleeves rolled up and sat on a bar stool to field unscripted questions from the audience. It was informal and cosy, but lacked the uplifting, crowd-pleasing patriotism of *Land of Hope and Glory*, the coloured balloons or the excitement of a staged rally. He said:

"I had been to the Gulf and been surrounded by soldiers and stood on tanks and talked to them. It was a hugely intimate gathering, although there were thousands of people there. It was like Greek theatre. My idea was to let anybody come to the meetings, anybody, and the security people and Central Office got hold of it and they said, firstly, somebody could kill you and, secondly, that I might get one or two hecklers and what television would show would not be 40 minutes of successful exchanges, but the one minute of heckling and difficulty. That's why they became ticket meetings and not the open ones I had originally envisaged. The national Press thought the questions were rigged – they weren't. I had no idea what the questions would be. But they attacked the idea, so, halfway through the election, I decided to get out my soapbox again."

Two trial runs in Bristol and York had been taped and studied and convinced John's advisers, who favoured a more formal meeting with questions screened in advance, it wasn't working. When they put their ideas to John, his reaction was summed up in two words: "Forget it."

In the end, he had to admit there was no way of knowing how his method would go down with a hostile crowd, but he was still determined to do things his way. When he tried the new campaign idea at Sawtry Village College, set in a village alongside the north-bound carriageway of the A1 between Huntingdon and Peterborough, even he began to see it as the soft option. One member of the audience was more concerned about the welfare of the England cricket team, who were in Australia, and hoped the Prime Minister could enlighten him.

A few days later, John reverted to more traditional electioneering with a walkabout in St Ives Market Square.

THE PRIVATE MAJOR

He declined to kiss any of the babies who were wheeled out on cue, but did some shopping, buying some steak in a butcher's shop and some salmon from a fishmongers.

If Norma was to join John on the campaign trail, she had to be certain that life at home would run smoothly. Maggie Scott, former owner of Slepe Hall Hotel in St Ives from 1970 to 1986 and a county councillor, was the woman behind Norma. It was her job to take care of all the little things, such as making sure there were enough eggs and bacon in the fridge at Finings. She would always have an umbrella at the ready if it looked like rain and a spare pair of shoes for aching feet at the end of the day. Maggie did things like organising the weekly shopping, making sure the children were taken care of and arranged Norma's hair appointments to fit in with the busy schedule. Now chairman of the Huntingdon Health Authority and the county council policy committee, she recalled:

"It was obvious from the time John became Chief Secretary to the Treasury that his commitments at Westminster and Norma's increased involvement in constituency work meant they could do with a bit of help. Of course, they didn't ask for it – their sense of responsibility is higher than anyone else's, so they just wouldn't. But they did need someone to liaise with family and friends, keep the domestic side of things together, little things that needed doing, and I volunteered to help. When John became PM, there hadn't been a wife at Number 10 for many years, so there was no support system set up for Norma. Weekends became very important for the family; weekends meaning from Saturday afternoon until about 6pm on Sunday, when John had to return to London. That time was precious and friends tried to make sure they had that time together."

About halfway through the 1992 campaign, those around John noticed a visible change in the way he approached the election. There were a few raised eyebrows in Huntingdon when the national campaign was launched, because people knew it just wasn't John Major's style of doing things. He said:

THE PRIVATE MAJOR

"I used to stand on a soapbox in Brixton to speak to people in the road outside the Conservative association and in the market. The story of the soapbox re-emerging was that a few days before I was due to speak in Luton, there had been a riot in Bolton and I was very frustrated because I wanted to get up and address the crowds, but the security people whisked Norma and I away. I was told it might be quite lively in Luton, so I put the soapbox in the back of the car in case it was. And it was. We got the soapbox out and it changed the nature of the campaign. It was hugely fun. It became alive. It wasn't one of these antiseptic occasions where people were held back behind barriers, you could shake hands with them and it became true flesh and blood politics."

"He's a street fighter," recalled John Bridge, then treasurer of the Huntingdon Association:

"The negative opinion polls and the doom and gloom just brought out the best in him. He performs even better in that kind of environment. On the night of the election we arrived at the St Ivo Centre, with all the Labour supporters adamant that we were going to get a 'bloody nose'. We watched the swing-ometer and listened to the gasps of surprise. People couldn't believe how wrong the media and the pollsters had been. We had no doubts about the Huntingdon vote because we had been out there and done the work."

Lady Blatch said:

"In the middle of the second week, John took over. He became much more materially involved with the planning and the direction of the campaign. He abandoned people's advice about 'don't go here and don't go there' and 'don't do this and don't do that'. He just ignored all of that, took his soap box out, talked to people straight, which was appealing and attractive. It was not unhelpful to have a Labour leader who was over-confident and took victory for granted. Neil Kinnock was going from soundbite to soundbite and Paddy Ashdown was wearing hard hats and standing on tops of cranes. When the historians look back they will see that John Major was personally responsible for winning that election, which we were losing until about half way through."

John said:

THE PRIVATE MAJOR

"I don't think anyone wins elections on their own. I think changing the campaign made a difference, but there were many complex reasons why that election turned out the way it did."

There was tight security in Huntingdon during the election campaign. The IRA had launched a bombing campaign. In London, there had been three bomb attacks in 48 hours. It all made the job of protecting the Prime Minister much more stressful.

The system for counting votes in the constituency was changed for the 1992 election. There were unsuccessful moves before the 1987 election to abandon the traditional Friday morning count in Huntingdon in favour of one the previous night, but district council officials knew this time that whichever way the national result went, John would be needed in London after the count.

The St Ivo Recreation Centre in St Ives was booked for the Thursday night. A room, with a large television screen, had been set aside for John to watch the national results as they came in. The counting would start around midnight and the declaration was expected at 3am, giving John enough time to make his acceptance speech and get back to Downing Street.

Although John and the campaign team had never doubted his support in Huntingdon, the 36,230 majority surprised everyone.

Nationally, fourteen and a half million people had voted for the Conservatives, the highest number of votes any Party had ever polled in an election. All through the campaign, John believed he would win by between 25-30 seats; in the end it was 21.

The tiny majority seriously hampered him and his efforts to see through his policies. Eventually this began to wear down his energy. Every vote in the Commons was a knife-edge situation. He had to be there all the time, late into the night, cajoling and meeting people, trying to persuade them to vote with the Government.

During that 1992 Parliament, Lady Blatch became a

THE PRIVATE MAJOR

Cabinet minister for a short time. John Patten, who was Secretary of State for Education became ill and Lady Blatch, as his minister, was asked to take over. She remembers:

"There was one occasion when we were all told to attend a secret Cabinet meeting at 6pm in John's room at the House of Commons. When that finished, we were told to come back at 11pm. I was scared out of my skin. This was the first week I had been secretary of state, unexpectedly, and here I was in my third Cabinet meeting of the day, with very high noon type politics. It was all terribly sombre and as we were walking out of the room in silence, John turned round and said: 'Why is it every time you come to a Cabinet meeting there's always trouble?' With that everybody laughed. It was right in the middle of the incredible Government falling scenario, but he knew how I was feeling and tried to lighten things up. The following week, I had to go to a Cabinet meeting myself and try to persuade them to support me. I made my speech and answered questions from people and eventually I got everyone to agree with me. John passed me a note across the table which read: 'I know it wasn't easy, but well done.'"

Having a Prime Minister living in the area is good for business, as many companies found out over the years. One which could base a large amount of its work on him was Mason's News Agency of Cambridge. Dave Moreau, who lives in Hemingford Grey, is a partner, and the man who had many dealings with national media interest in his MP. He said:

"John Major's rapid rise to power seemed to catch everyone, including us, slightly off guard. I remember visiting his house one night after he joined the Cabinet and not being able to get an answer when I knocked on the front door.
"The only security then was a blue van on the edge of the drive, containing only the policemen detailed to look after the VIP. They nearly all had heart attacks when I knocked on their window in pitch dark.
"On the night he became Prime Minister, I found myself in front of a television with Mr Major's friends and relatives at the old Conservative

Club, The Views. I was working for Sky News and the national newspapers and managed to get several exclusive interviews that night — I think I was the only journalist who knew where Huntingdon was, let alone what his family looked like.

"John Major was good business for this agency. Regularly, we planned our Fridays around faxes and phone calls from Peter Brown. Our reporter Bobby Mullineaux and photographer Geoff Robinson became the most familiar faces at the constituency scrums. Our television interviews were regularly re-sold to national and international stations.

"Inevitably, too, there was interest in his family. Norma Major quite obviously had difficulty adapting to the modern 'first lady' demands, and the national newspapers demanded details of friends and social life.

"There was James Major, his football and his girlfriends. James was always decent to deal with and until the popular Sunday newspapers for involved in his love life, I felt he enjoyed the coverage. Liz Major was intensely shy and only occasionally featured, most notably when she fell off a horse during a charity race at Huntingdon Racecourse.

"On the whole, we did our job by covering Mr Major's public engagements and keeping an eye on the family for anything that had obviously become the subject of public discussion. Almost inevitably, as the pressure was turned on the Majors, it was hard for their friends to accept the media exposure. Despite that, I can look back and say we did more to prevent intrusion into their family life than we did to encourage it.

"If anyone wants to argue that point, I could tell them a few of the stories that never made the papers!"

The latter half of 1992, saw John and the Conservative Party plunged to previously unrecorded depths of unpopularity.

The turmoil over the Exchange Rate Mechanism (ERM) – some were calling the move to let the pound float freely a brave one, others viewed it as damaging U-turn – finally came to a head on "Black Wednesday" in September. Britain's membership of the ERM was suspended, devaluing the pound by 10 per cent. In a frantic attempt to keep the pound afloat, the Bank of England lost £10 billion of tax payers' money.

THE PRIVATE MAJOR

There was pressure on the Chancellor, Norman Lamont, to resign and John was now, according to the opinion polls, the most unpopular Prime Minster since records began. At the Party Conference in October, rows over European policy brought about calls for his resignation.

Then stories about the private lives of his ministers started hitting the headlines. John seemed to be limping from one crisis to the next and losing popularity and credibility on a daily basis.

Cyril Bridge believes:

"When you select people to the Cabinet, you give them an extra special job, because that's what it is, and some of them weren't even loyal to him.

"You can understand the electorate going away, all the sleaze and the back-biting, people don't like that sort of thing."

John says at this time and later when things became worse, he did everything he could to bring the Party together and heal the rifts.

"I tried everything that could be done, from private meetings and discussions to lengthy discussions and meetings with the 1922 Committee about the strategic impact on the Conservative Party. I don't know what could conceivably have been done that I didn't do. The trouble is they all wanted me to change a policy into a direction that they thought was right and I didn't and I wasn't prepared to do that . . . so it went on."

ORDINARY PEOPLE

While John Major apparently concentrated on European policy during the latter part of 1992 and early 1993, things began to turn sour. Unemployment was rising, the housing market had still not recovered from the slump of the late 1980s and the Government's economic polices seemed, by most people's standards, to be failing. In June of 1993, Norman Lamont, the Chancellor of the Exchequer, resigned and with echoes of Geoffrey Howe's damning Commons speech in 1990, which instigated the downfall of Margaret Thatcher, he launched a bitter attack on John in the House.

Mr Lamont's "in office, but not in power," accusation stunned the Commons and public alike. But the green shoots of economic recovery were beginning to sprout up in John's own backyard. A 30 per cent leap in the number of people setting up businesses in Huntingdonshire was welcome, but the garden was definitely not rosy.

Even in the constituency, his popularity seemed to be slipping. A survey, carried out in Huntingdon High Street during the summer of 1993, showed that only half those interviewed thought the Prime Minister should continue in office. It was fairly comforting, however, compared to national opinion polls, which showed that 86 per cent of the population wanted him to stand down.

The decision in October, 1992, announced by Michael Heseltine, to close 31 pits, with the loss of 30,000 mining jobs, was greeted with widespread outrage. The miners, their families and a large section of the media all accused the Prime Minister of caring more about Europe than ordinary working class people in his own country.

THE PRIVATE MAJOR

John said:

"I wasn't immersed in Europe, but I did miss the mines situation. I knew the weekend before the announcement, as I paced up and down my kitchen, that it was going to cause a huge fuss, but all logic said we had no choice but to do it. All the advice we got said the miners were expecting it and wanted the uncertainty ended. I felt uneasy with it, but to have changed the policy would have cost hundreds of millions of pounds extra every month, so there was no rational reason for doing it, other than an instinct which said it wasn't quite right. In retrospect, it wasn't quite right and I should have taken my instinct more seriously. I should have let my heart rule my head."

Speculation over John's future as Prime Minister and calls for an autumn election hung heavily in the air.

The national newspapers had varying opinions about what he should do. The publications which were not encouraging him to resign included *The Daily Express*, which described him as: "decent and honourable," and urged him to prove Mr Lamont wrong. *The Daily Telegraph* wrote: "Conservatives are baying and tearing at each other in a fashion that may yet undo them all." *The Daily Star* offered John the following advice: "Take a big stick and whack the disloyal, bickering Party into line." John said:

"People forget that Governments govern by delivering a majority. Without a majority in the House of Commons, Governments fall, so we had to persuade people we were right and it was immensely time-consuming and often quite heart-rending to do so."

When it came to criticism, there was no-one more capable of reducing grown men to quivering wrecks than Connie Jeffrey. As *The Hunts Post* village correspondent for Great Stukeley from 1993 to 1995 and a near neighbour of John and Norma, Connie felt well placed to add her rhetoric to that already written about the Prime Minister.

Those who have witnessed her sharp tongue and even sharper pen wish never to repeat the experience. The white-haired pensioner, who refuses to divulge her age, was a regular letter writer to the local papers during the Prime Minister's formative years, although what appeared in print had usually been heavily edited for the sake of taste, decency and legal soundness.

One letter, printed in June, 1993, read: "Until recently, I had regarded the Prime Minister with a kind of amused contempt, indeed for a lad with two O-Levels under his belt, he has made remarkable progress. Now, I am thanking my lucky stars that he didn't get three. It's mind-boggling to contemplate what he might have achieved."

She saw herself as the champion of pensioners' causes.

When Michael Portillo, or Putrid Portillo, as Connie called him, announced plans to increase prescription charges, she launched a bitter attack. "If enough pensioners die because they can't afford the increases, the financial situation will be resolved in one stroke," she quipped.

When the corner shop in Great Stukeley closed down, Connie knew who was to blame.

"If he and Norma had used it more, the owners wouldn't have gone out of business. Local people would have gone in there just to see Norma buying her *Woman's Weekly* or whatever it is she reads," she thundered.

When John was on a walkabout in Huntingdon High Street during the 1992 election campaign, Connie saw her opportunity to lambast him over the rise in business rates. She said:

"I walked up to him, pointed my finger and said: 'What are you going to do about the business rate?' People just stood there with their mouths open, they couldn't believe that anyone in Huntingdon would dare to criticise John Major in public."

Over the years, Connie's letters and comments to the local papers attracted national media attention. She often received a mention in the columns of *The Guardian* and Jeremy Paxman interviewed her on *Newsnight*.

Requests for interviews were now a daily occurrence for

THE PRIVATE MAJOR

John, whose routine had become punishing. He would get up at about 6am at Downing Street, have a bath, then work on official boxes for an hour.

At 8.30am, there would be a meeting with his junior ministers and his private secretary and a Cabinet meeting at 10.30am. During the late morning and early afternoon, there would be meetings with various secretaries of state. From 4pm-5pm he worked on speeches and then met Sarah Hogg, his policy adviser, for an hour.

There would usually be another meeting during the early evening, before some kind of function or business dinner later. When he returned to the flat at Downing Street, he usually had to work on boxes before finally climbing into bed. He said:

"There was this ludicrous story of me being lonely and stuck at the top of Downing Street on my own, because Norma was in Huntingdon. It was complete rubbish. Lots of people have a kitchen Cabinet of cronies, but I didn't think you could do that when you may be called upon to sack them. How can you put yourself in a position where you've had a close relationship with someone, discussing problems even though he or she may need to be removed? You are then personally obliged and can't remove them. I didn't have any people like that in Government and that means you haven't particularly got people to turn to. There were people who very good friends. Douglas Hurd, successive chiefs whips and Michael Heseltine, while he was deputy Prime Minister. Many people thought there would be difficulties with Michael and I working together. That wasn't true, working with Michael Heseltine for that last couple of years was one of the happiest working relationships I ever had."

Norma also scoffs at any suggestions of her husband being a lonely figure at any time. She said:

"People don't seem to realise you can get in a car in Huntingdon and an hour-and-a-half later, you can be in Downing Street. I was actually there a lot more than many people realise. Many times, though, I would attend a dinner function, but then have to be back for an early start in Huntingdon. I was like a yo-yo up and down between

Huntingdon and London. John was home most weekends."

John Bridge said:

"Everything is focused on the top man. From a constituency point of view, we were not expecting the intensity and the continuous spotlight on him. Having seen him rise up and take the top jobs, we thought we were prepared, but there is a huge difference between even Chancellor and Prime Minister. Whenever there was some sort of so-called crisis, we would be called upon to give interviews. The media always wanted a constituency perspective. We were always happy to talk and chat, but made it clear that we were not going to break any confidences or give them any information about Norma or the children."

Many Conservatives in Huntingdon have experienced acts of kindness shown by Norma, which were all the more appreciated when John became Prime Minister because of the constraints on her time. Norma has been known to sit by hospital bedsides, with someone who is ill, for hours and never forgets to show her appreciation when people have helped her or John. After each election, she would personally go round and thank staff and helpers for their support. Cyril Bridge recalled:

"My son-in-law, who had served in the Gulf War, had been presented with a white Bible which he asked me to get Norma to sign. I gave it to her and she said: 'Leave it with me'. She had it for ages and, well, I didn't like to ask for it back. Every so often she would say: 'It's all right, I haven't forgotten'. I knew I would get it back some time, but when I did about three months later Norma said: 'I'm sorry to have kept it for so long, but there are one or two other names in there'. My son-in-law is an American airman. He couldn't believe it when he saw that George Bush had signed it. Norma had taken it to all the functions and dinners she was asked to attend in that three months and got all these heads of state to sign it."

Peter Brown marvelled at how John was able to bring "the common touch" to everything he dealt with, despite the

THE PRIVATE MAJOR

pressure. He said:

"There is nothing false about John Major — what you see is what you get. His modesty, charm and kindness are qualities which shine through to everyone who meets him. People who meet him for the first time always say something like: 'If only he came over on television like he did when . . .' That's why I believe if we could get him into every lounge in the country, we would be home and dry. He's got this ability to relate to people and it's something he doesn't have to work on, it's a gift. We have had national Press people here trying to rake up bad things to say about him, but they always left empty-handed. So, in some ways, my job has been easy, because I don't have to go around defending him or explain what he's doing, because he does that so well himself. On the other hand, it is more difficult, because so many people want to see him. He's an amazing character."

John has often became embroiled in local issues because people thought he could smooth the path of their particular grievance or put in a good word.

When a telephone box in the village of Hemingford Grey became the focus of national media attention in the March of 1994, he was instructed by some local residents to: "Keep your nose out."

A family in the village had written to John, in his capacity as MP, to complain about night-time noise around a telephone box in Church Street. They asked him if he could help in their fight to get it moved. John wrote a letter to Sir Ian Valance, the chairman of British Telecom, asking him to review the matter and walked into unexpected controversy.

Several parish councillors threatened to resign if the kiosk was moved an inch. A petition against siting it somewhere else was supported by 381 people. Eventually the phone box stayed put.

Then there were some people in the constituency who felt the relationship between some local Conservatives and John and Norma was just a little bit too cosy.

In November, 1994, Pree Newbon, who was chairman of

82

THE PRIVATE MAJOR

Huntingdonshire District Council's planning committee, was brought before the Local Government Ombudsman to explain her friendship with Norma.

Mrs Newbon's casting vote secured the approval of a £500,000 Mencap home in Orchard Lane in Huntingdon, and she faced a barrage of criticism.

The scheme, which had initially been rejected by district councillors, was revised and resubmitted to the planning committee. Local residents, who were objecting to the plan because they felt it was too cramped, said she should have declared her friendship with Norma as a personal interest in the matter.

After she was cleared by the Local Government Ombudsman she said: "My interests in John and Norma were zero as far as this scheme was concerned. Of course, I knew them, every Conservative councillor knows them, but there was no substance in this case."

The Views, which had been the headquarters of the Huntingdon Conservative Association for more than two decades, faced closure in 1994.

Membership plummeted from 1000 to just 200, leaving the club with debts of around £10,000. The falling membership was blamed on the rise in subscriptions which had doubled to £20 the previous year. Although the possibility of extending membership to non-party members was considered, a rival bid to buy the club by another political party was dismissed. Local Liberal Democrat leader Percy Meyer said: "We may wish to take it off their hands."

John Bridge said the situation at The Views was not a political one, although some elements of the media had tried to turn it into one. He said:

"That was all about the changing social lives of people. People were much more conscious of drink-driving and social clubs all over the place were struggling. In the case of The Views, it was in the middle of Huntingdon, serving a largely rural constituency. People were not prepared to drive there for an evening out. The Views is run independently of the association, but we helped out by helping them

83

find the right people to help improve matters and gave financial
assistance which enabled them to continue in the way they felt was
right."

The Views, situated between the railway station and town
centre, continued as a Conservative club until the summer
of 1997. It is currently for sale, with offers being invited in
the region of £400,000, with agents Barford saying it has
scope to be developed into offices or leisure activities.
Alternatively, it may go back to being a home.

Although John had managed to fend off calls for an early
election during the autumn of 1992 and again during the
following two terms, the rifts over Europe within the
Conservative Party had become an ever-widening gap. By
the summer of 1995, he knew it would be impossible for him
to continue in office unless he quelled the rising rebellion
from his own backbenches. He said:

"There were disputes and huge civil wars within the Party over
European policy that went on for a very long time. It wasn't a very
edifying spectacle and this really began to undermine everything we
were prepared to do. In the end, I decided that if they didn't like what I
was doing and they wanted somebody else, they had better have the
opportunity to say so. As I put it in the garden at Downing Street: 'Put
up or shut up.'"

John's decision on June 22 to resign as leader of the
Conservative Party was regarded by some as the greatest
piece of political manoeuvring this century.

It wasn't so much an act of mastery as a desperate bid to
reaffirm his leadership. He had reached the end of the road
with his divided and disloyal Party. The prospect of the
bickering carrying on through the next three months and
up until the Party conference in October was too much for
him to bear. It would have been five more months of
squabbling, which he knew would dominate the media. Far
better to settle the matter once and for all.

84

PUT UP OR SHUT UP

THERE was a certain satisfaction for John Major as he sat back and watched the reaction to his shock decision to resign as leader of the Conservative Party reverberating around the world.

Once he had made up his mind, John had no doubts that he was doing the right thing. He was fed up with the "nonsense" of the past three years, and thought it was time to put an end to it. He said:

"I had been thinking about what I would do for some time. I pretty much made up my mind the weekend before, but finally made up my mind, absolutely, definitely, on the Wednesday. It's frustrating when you are not able to do precisely what you want when you are considering whether you should do something or not. I don't spend time agitating and worrying over a decision, I get on having made that decision.

"I'm an Airean . . . if you want to do something, you want to get on and do it. I'd made up my mind it was the right thing to do and I was anxious to get on and do it."

He says he "vaguely" talked it through with Douglas Hurd and Chancellor of the Exchequer Ken Clarke on the plane on the way back from the G7 Conference of industrialised powers in Halifax, Nova Scotia, a few days before, but had already decided what he was going to do. He said:

"I didn't really discuss whether I should do it with anyone. No-one else could make that decision. I got quite a lot of advice from people, who, when they were told, would have preferred me not to do it, but by that stage, I wasn't going to be deterred."

85

THE PRIVATE MAJOR

The only person he talked everything through with was Norma. He told her the magical number of votes he wanted in order to remain in office and says, to this day, neither of them has told another soul what that figure was. He said:

"I won't tell anyone else until my book; I want to save something for that!"

Technically, to win outright he needed to secure the votes of at least half the 329 Conservative MPs entitled to vote. He also had to be 50 votes ahead of his nearest rival. He could win with 165 votes, but less than 200 would destroy his credibility, as over one third of Conservative MPs would have failed to give him their support.

The night before the resignation, June 21, 1995, he told "one or two" of his Cabinet colleagues of his decision, but the following day at Cabinet, he remained tight-lipped. Other members of the Cabinet were told afterwards. At 4.15pm, after Prime Minister's Questions, he summoned the 1922 Executive Committee and told them what he proposed to do.

He says: "They were a touch surprised . . . to put it mildly." All 18 members pledged their support for him, although some would later go back on their word. He said:

"Many people thought I would lose at the outset. There was certainly a possibility that I would lose. I don't think there was a possibility that I would physically lose, and that somebody else would get more votes than me, but what was a possibility was that my opponents would get a sufficiently large enough number of votes for me to decide that I couldn't carry on. That was the real danger."

As he walked to the Downing Street garden in the dappled sunlight, he felt as though a weight had been lifted off his shoulders. It was almost possible to feel the anticipation in the air as he approached the rostrum. The media had been told the Prime Minister was making an announcement at 5pm and had gathered accordingly. As he prepared to make his speech, the only sounds to be heard were the clicking of cameras and the faint rustling of notepaper. He said:

"Let me just make a brief statement to you. I've been deeply involved in politics since I was 16. I see public service as a duty and if you can serve, I believe you have an obligation to do so. I've now been Prime Minister for nearly five years. In that time we've achieved a great deal, but for the last three, I've been opposed by a small minority in our Party. During those three years there have been repeated threats of a leadership election. In each year, they turned out to be phoney threats. Now the same thing again is happening in 1995. I believe it is in no-one's interest that this continues right through until November. It undermines the Government and it damages the Conservative Party. I am not prepared to see the Party I care for laid out on the rack like this any longer. To remove this uncertainty, I have this afternoon tendered my resignation as leader of the Conservative Party to Sir Marcus Fox, the chairman of the 1922 Committee, and requested him to set the machinery in motion for an election for a successor. I have confirmed to Sir Marcus that I shall be a candidate in that election. If I win, I shall continue as Prime Minister and lead the Party into and through the next General Election. Should I be defeated, which I do not expect, I shall resign as Prime Minister and offer my successor my full support. The Conservative Party must make its choice. Every leader is leader only with the support of his Party. That is true of me as well. This is why I am no longer prepared to tolerate the present situation. In short, it is time to put up or shut up. I have nothing more to say this afternoon. Thank you very much."

Norma and James Major were standing on the terrace at Number 10 watching the proceedings. James had taken a day off from his job as a trainee manger at Marks and Spencer in Norwich to be with his father. Norma said:

"The Press were all sitting there below us and there was an incredible air of expectation because only a very few people knew what he was going to say. I had to be there because it was history in the making. The fact that the Press knew nothing about it was absolutely fantastic. It was a wonderful moment."

Norma denies she wanted her husband to take himself

87

THE PRIVATE MAJOR

out of the firing line. She said:

"I was laid back about it. I didn't want it to end, because there was still a job for John to do."

John was the first Conservative leader to resign in such circumstances since the Party rules were changed in 1974 to allow for annual elections. Most Conservatives were confident that the leadership election, due to take place on July 4, would be a one-horse race. Surely no-one would oppose him and even if they did, it wouldn't be a serious challenge?

But some of John's colleagues and friends were not at all surprised when Welsh Secretary John Redwood lifted his head above the parapet a few days later. Lady Blatch had been listening to the back-biting within the Party for months. She knew it was getting worse and the momentum was gathering, so she decided to approach John on the Sunday before he made his announcement and tell him what was going on. He said:

"I probably knew more than he did at the time, I was hearing all the disgruntles and the terrible things that were being said. I went over to see him on the Sunday morning to talk to him. I thought he needed to know what was going on and I wanted to talk some ideas through with him. I knew he needed to take things by the throat. We sat in the garden and chatted and then walked around the garden and talked. He was very pensive and thoughtful. He didn't over-respond much or say: 'Yes, I know all this and I know what I should be doing.' He was just listening and taking account. He never ever did confide that he was going to resign. We just talked as two friends, but he knew and I knew that he couldn't go on. He was being undermined quite openly and blatantly. It was just awful and making life absolutely intolerable for him.

"On the Thursday, I was summoned to Lord Cranborne's office at 4pm. He said: 'There's a special announcement being made to do with the Prime Minister.' My first thought was that John was going to resign as Prime Minister. I was as new to what happened in the garden that day as anybody else was. I don't believe my chat with him on that

THE PRIVATE MAJOR

Sunday morning influenced him in any way, I think he was already mulling all of it through and realising he had to turn around to our Party and say: 'Back me or sack me'. I thought the way he did it was outstanding. It was a very courageous thing to do because he could have gone down with a very big wallop at that stage. If one had converted all the malicious chatter that was going on into votes, one wouldn't have expected him to win the contest. I've always thought, I thought it then and I still think it now, that it was a good thing he was challenged by a heavyweight like John Redwood because if he'd only been challenged by a stalking horse, people would have said anyone can beat a stalking horse. But to beat a real challenger was important. It was all part of the stresses and strains of having no working majority and trying to keep the show on the road. I think he had to be nearly superhuman to get through that."

When John Bridge took over from Mike Harford as chairman of the Huntingdon Conservative Association in January, 1995, he knew it was going to be a difficult year.

The Boundary Commission had redrawn the Huntingdon constituency lines again, effectively dumping a further 24,000 potential voters. The market town of Ramsey and the villages of Earith, Sawtry, Stilton and Bluntisham moved into the new North-west Cambridgeshire constituency and St Neots and Buckden returned to the Huntingdon fold. Some Huntingdon Association members couldn't bear the prospect of not being able to vote for John at the next election. John Bridge said:

"A lot of people were very upset, they couldn't comprehend the fact that they would no longer be part of the constituency. It was a very difficult period for us."

When the phone rang at 4.45pm in the office of C W Bridge, the family haulage business in St Peter's Road, Huntingdon, on June 22, John Bridge found out what a difficult period really felt like.

The call his secretary put through was from Peter Brown. There was to be an announcement in the next few minutes that the Prime Minister was resigning as leader of the party.

John Bridge put the phone down, called his wife Jenny at home to say he would be late and then cancelled a meeting he had planned to attend that evening at Great Stukeley Village Hall. Immediately after his second call, the phone rang. It was BBC Radio Cambridgeshire, they wanted an interview. That first request was followed by several more from radio stations, including BBC Radio Four, who said "you're live on air, Mr Bridge" just before asking the opening question.

In between the radio interviews and answering questions from newspaper reporters, he did manage to ring his wife and say: "Can you put my dinner in the oven, I'm appearing on the 9pm news." He recalled:

"When Peter Brown phoned, he was very positive and that was the message I tried to pass on to the association members. We trusted John's judgement. He had surprised people before, and we were all fed up with what had been going on. A lot of people put themselves before the Party, which was the legacy of the Thatcher Government. A selfish culture developed and it came back and bit us."

When John Bridge returned home that evening, Jenny was frantic. She had spent all evening taking calls from journalists. He says they both realised that night what kind of pressure John and Norma were under every day.

On the Friday, it was business as usual in Huntingdon. Leadership election or not, it was a constituency day. During the day, John visited Needingworth Primary School, The Ailwyn School in Ramsey and Huntingdon Community Radio.

The radio station, which was broadcasting on a 28-day trial basis, was based above a betting office in the main High Street, an irony not lost on the journalists who had been door-stepping the Prime Minister all morning.

One asked if he was going to place a bet on the leadership election. As John walked round the studio, his security staff passed him pieces of paper to read at regular intervals. It turned out not to be news of a stalking horse or even a serious contender for his job, but the latest cricket score from Lord's.

He agreed to give an exclusive interview to *The Hunts Post* and as there was nowhere to sit in a side room, off the main corridor, he perched on the end of a desk, and said:

"I think people all around the country will think it was time to sort this matter out and settle everything down. I feel that very strongly. I think whether people agree with me or not, they will think it's the right thing to do."

After talking about the reasons behind his decision to resign, he chatted about Norma and the children and then turned his thoughts to his garden at Finings:

"We've just built a pond in the garden and it's nearly finished. We have put some fish it in, but the water has gone a bit murky so I'm not too sure if they're still alive."

In the next few days, there were almost as many column inches written about the pond as the leadership election.

That weekend, when Cyril Bridge saw John he told him:

"I said, 'John what are you doing?' He shrugged, smiled and said: 'It'll be all right, I shall win'."

Three days later, John Redwood resigned from the Cabinet and announced his decision to oppose John. The contest had begun.

The Huntingdon Conservative faithful were gathered at The Views to wait for the result of the ballot on July 4.

The patio doors at one end of the long ground floor room had been opened to allow journalists and television crews access and let some fresh air in.

It was a warm evening and the room was packed. A clock on the wall seemed to be ticking at an annoyingly slow pace, oblivious to the urgency of the proceedings. Every so often, a mobile phone would bleep and shatter people's concentration.

The occasional glass of gin and tonic was helping to calm the nerves of some people. When the result came through on a television in the corner of the room, a deafening cheer went up.

It was so loud that it was impossible for the reporters present to hear the result and other details of the vote. To the people in the room, none of that mattered. He'd done enough to silence the doubters and settle the matter down, for now, at least.

John Major received 218 votes to John Redwood's 89, and there were 10 abstentions and 12 spoiled papers.

"Never had any doubt that he would come through," said party member and local councillor Pree Newbon. But had he done enough?

"A win is a win," retorted Ruth Clapham, chairman of the St Neots Conservative Association. "The MPs who didn't vote for John Major have missed an opportunity to do the right thing. They are traitors," she spat.

Association president Mike Harford said: "I had no doubt that Mr Major would get the result we all wanted. Now I hope we can now go down the road of unity. The last few days have been such a strain for John and Norma."

Peter Brown admitted the contest had been: "quite a headache," for John.

A few days later, Labour leader Jim Lomax said: "It's a good result for the Labour Party because he will go down at the next election." Percy Meyer, leader of the Liberal Democrats quipped: "It's like 218 turkeys voting for Christmas, because many of them will lose their seats at the next election."

In reflection, John admits the events of July 1995 were only partially successful, but believes things would have been much worse without the leadership election. He said:

THE PRIVATE MAJOR

"People who felt very strongly about the European debate on both sides just went on and on. It didn't wholly work, but it was undoubtedly better than it would have otherwise been."

His victory should have given him a platform on which to start building for the next election. But there were still those in the Party who had not forgiven him for Maastricht and were not about to give up now. Lady Blatch said:

"He was not even given credit for the good things he got out of Maastricht. They just used anything they could as a stick with which to beat him over the head. There was a lot of backbench disgruntlement, people began to get nervous because they could see the election looming and the Party was so split. They thought: 'If only we could change the leader now' everything will be all right. There were some who thought his leadership was weak, but others were just being talked into this mind set of: 'If we get rid of him now, we've still got a year or 18 months to pull the Party round'. It was shades of that thinking that had got rid of Margaret Thatcher. People thought: 'That worked out all right in the end, we can do it again'. There were others who were quietly staying by John and being loyal to him, but they weren't the ones being vocal. What we heard and the public heard, right up until the '97 election, was the rebellion and not the support."

10

FINAL CURTAIN

BY the time the 1997 election was announced for May 1, the Conservative Party was in disarray. The Tory rebels had refused to toe the Party line and were still "causing trouble", according to Lady Blatch, who said:

"The perception in people's minds was that we were a sleazy and disunited Party and that was a very powerful disincentive to keep us in office."

The Labour Party leader, Tony Blair, in contrast, looked exciting and fresh and, above all, in control. The New Labour election slogan gave out the right message to the electorate who were now bored with Conservative misfortunes.

A lot of Conservatives believed it would need a minor miracle to pull off election success this time around. John Major admits he had resigned himself to defeat before May 1, but was determined to rally the troops and achieve the best possible vote. He said:

"I thought it was very unlikely that we would win, for two reasons. Firstly, we had been there for 18 years and secondly because the Labour Party hadn't made the mistakes necessary to enable us to stretch democratic tolerance for a further election. If the Labour Party had made some very bad mistakes during the election campaign, conceivably we might have won. If the Conservative Party had behaved itself in the campaign, and if the electorate had seen the Labour Party falling apart, we might have won.

"We went into the campaign with the best economy of any Government in my lifetime. In terms of the economy and industrial

94

THE PRIVATE MAJOR

prosperity, we had a very good story to tell, better than any
Government in living memory, but because they weren't any economic
problems, people weren't focused on them, so you needed the Labour
Party to make mistakes.

"I knew we had a very large hill to climb. You can't concentrate on
the economy with MPs playing ducks and drakes with the national
manifesto. It just knocked us off. Every time we got on to something
that was a productive electoral position, we got knocked off by some
extraneous event, like someone making their own statement about the
single currency or whatever. If those things hadn't happened, the
election result would have been a lot closer."

During the campaign, several damaging stories appeared:
one which said the Conservatives would cut pensions, and
another alerting the public to the Party's intention to
privatise health. Both were instantly and angrily denied,
but the doubt inflicted on an already sceptical electorate
just made the job of trying to convince people to vote
Conservative even harder. By this time, John felt more and
more that his Party were unlikely to win. He said:

"It's hard to explain unless you are in the middle of an election
campaign, but a feeling comes through. There were several moments
when I was sure there were not sufficient votes to win."

Norma was with John throughout the campaign, working
tirelessly right up to the count, as she has done at every
election. She said:

"We have done so many campaigns over the years and I was
involved from day one. I look back now and think I might have spent
more time with my mother, because within a month of the election,
she was dead. This one wasn't any more punishing than the others,
although it was much longer. But we got a tremendous reception
wherever we went and lots of things were happening. People keep
you going, but I cannot say that it wasn't exacting."

At 9.30am on polling day, John cast his vote at Great
Stukeley Village Hall. He told reporters: "It's a very good

omen for democracy when you've got weather like this on polling day." He and Norma appeared relaxed and confident in the bright sunshine, even though they had logged thousands of miles on the campaign trail during the previous six weeks.

John's decision to make it the longest campaign in modern political history was made for two reasons. He explained:

"One was that I was absolutely certain the Labour Party and the Liberals would try and bring up sleaze and dredge it into the campaign as much as they could. I thought they would be able to keep it going for a week, so I wanted to get that out of the way and concentrate on the real issues. As it happened, members of my Party contributed to make sure it carried on rather longer. The second was that I thought the longer the Labour Party was exposed to a General Election the more possible it was that people would begin to ask serious questions of them; in that I was proved wrong. The most serious question most members of the Labour Party were asked during the election was: 'Tell us what's wrong with the Tories today.' They were not asked the critical questions."

Ever since she first voted in 1929, Matilda Barlow had put an *X* beside the name of the Conservative Party candidate. At lunchtime on polling day, the 101-year-old was sitting on a bench outside the Axe and Compass pub in Hemingford Abbots when the Prime Minister came over for a chat. Mrs Barlow, who had moved to the village four years previously from Manchester, declined a postal vote, preferring to make a personal appearance at the polling station. She had been ready since 7am and had worn her best navy blue dress for the occasion. She told reporters:

"I'm quite ready to die now I've voted for the Prime Minister. He has done a marvellous job for the Party. He had a difficult job following Mrs Thatcher and he has worked extremely hard. He's a lovely man."

The media looked on in amusement as she offered the

Prime Minister her glass of port and lemon. He took a sip before handing it back to her and sat and chatted for some time as he downed half a pint of lager.

At 1pm, John and Norma returned to Finings. There were about a dozen people there, including Jeffrey Archer, John Bridge and Peter Brown. Lady Blatch and John sat at a table on the patio eating their lunch. It was a beautiful day, the warm sun and the water gently spilling out of the fountain in the garden pond creating a peaceful setting. Meanwhile, the slaughter at the polls continued. John Bridge said:

"We knew eventually his term as PM would come to an end, but we would never have wished it to have happened in such a way. He was still going around the committee rooms on polling day, smiling and thanking people, treating them like they were long lost friends. He was busy motivating people and driving them on. He did not pass on any of his anguish at any point."

The news that everyone had been expecting came at about 6pm. The early exit polls confirmed the worst. Lady Blatch said:

"John was good company and we didn't talk about it a lot. We didn't go around crying on each other's shoulders at that point. It was all fairly relaxed. We were all not wanting to broach the subject too much. It was only later during the evening that the scale of it started to hit him."

When John and Norma were driven to the Burgess Hall, part of the St Ivo Recreation Centre in St Ives, where the count was held, John had already began formulating things in his mind that evening. He says by polling day he was: "stone cold certain" that the Conservatives would not win the election.

"I was thinking more about the people I knew and had worked with in Parliament, very good MPs, who had lost their seats. That was on my

THE PRIVATE MAJOR

mind – many of them were old friends. The next day, we would have to see the Downing Street staff and say goodbye. You're saying goodbye to people you have worked closely with for a long time.

"Politics has never been the only thing in my life, so I concentrated on other matters. In the short-term I had to become leader of the opposition, deal with the Queen's speech, Prime Minister's Questions, arrange the appointment of a shadow Cabinet and liaise with the 1922 Committee, and we had to find somewhere else to live in London. I didn't sit in the corner thinking about it . . . life goes on."

Lady Blatch, along with James and Elizabeth Major, joined John and Norma in a little side room at the Burgess Hall that evening. There was a television in the corner of the room and they all sat around listening to the last results to come through. Hardly anyone spoke, instead using looks and gestures to convey their thoughts and feelings. Several people told John not to blame himself and reminded him that the electorate had wanted changed after 18 years of Tory rule. Lady Blatch said:

"The thing that hit him hard and really did hurt was to see people like Ian Lang and Malcolm Rifkind on the screen and suddenly the count would come on. Losing elections is always terrible, but losing really good people, and not because they were bad MPs is sad. But in this election, people who had worked hard in their constituencies were just swept away on a tide. That I know hurt, it really did hurt. There were no tears, but I just knew the reality and the enormity of the loss came through, seeing really good friends lose their seats and other backbenchers who were not thought to be in danger at that election.

"I don't know how I could have handled that afterwards, having to make a speech and face the media. He stood on the platform and used the right number of words to say what he needed to say. He said it was a difficult night for the Tory Party and thanked the people he needed to thank, and then had to go off to London and face the public scrutiny there. He didn't actually have to go back to Downing Street the next day, but he wanted to come out of that front door and do it properly and not skulk around somewhere."

John sat and watched the political map of Great Britain

98

gradually turn red. After 18 years in charge of the nation, the Conservative defeat broke all modern political records. The Party lost a quarter of its 1992 vote, a third of its Cabinet ministers and half of its seats. In Scotland and Wales, it was wiped off the map and there were no Tory MPs representing any major city, with the exception of Sutton Coldfield in the West Midlands and the wealthier parts of London. The number of Conservative MPs who returned to Parliament was the lowest since 1906. Norma said she had accepted defeat well before May 1. She said:

"I felt it was inevitable. We had been in power for too long. If anybody had said any Party would be in power for 18 years, you would say it was impossible, but we had done it. The Party behaved very badly and people wanted a change. We made it safe for people to vote Labour."

John said:

"You cannot be angry at democracy. It was democracy which made the Conservative Party. It was democracy which made me Prime Minister. You cannot be angry if democracy changes its mind."

Many Conservatives had accepted the likelihood of election defeat on May 1, but few could have imagined the scale of the Labour landslide. Lady Blatch said:

"I had canvassed all over the country and we knew in our bones that we were going to lose. People on the doorstep were holding back on us. They were quiet and solemn. We always knew it would be tough, but none of us counted on the scale. In terms of seats, it was completely and utterly devastating."

The Conservatives did actually manage to poll more votes in the 1992 election than Labour did on May 1, 1997. Lady Blatch explained:

"Four and a half million people who voted Conservative in 1992 did not vote Conservative in 1997 and two million of those stayed at

99

home. We believe they were our votes, the people who weren't convinced enough to vote Labour or Liberal, but were unhappy with us. The Referendum Party and the UK Independence Party took a significant amount of votes, a lot of whom were almost certainly Tory sceptics. We actually lost between a million and a million-and-a-half votes. The Referendum Party took 17 of our seats. People lost their seats because of the splitting of the vote."

As expected, John did well in Huntingdon. There were 24,000 less voters than at the 1992 election, because of boundary changes, but he still managed to increase his percentage of the vote.

He polled 31,501 votes, which gave him a majority of 18,140. Labour's Jason Reece was second with 13,361; Matthew Owen (Lib Dem) 8390; high profile candidate Professor David Bellamy (Ref Party) 3114; Charles Coyne (UK Ind) 331; Veronica Hufford (Christian Dem) 177 and Duncan Robertson 89.

Just before the declaration, Elizabeth Major and her boyfriend Luke, along with James Major and his then girlfriend Elaine, walked into the hall. They all seemed to be desperately seeking friendly faces, refusing to make eye contact with journalists. There was a lethargic atmosphere in the Burgess Hall. It was now just after 3am, and any anticipation or faint hope that John just might confound his critics once more and pull off another spectacular victory had evaporated hours ago.

The reporters, photographers and camera crews, who had arrived at 7pm, to be assured of a space near the stage, were tired, fed up and cold. Some photographers were complaining bitterly. They knew unless something dramatic happened in the next few minutes their pictures would be worthless. It was Tony Blair and New Labour who would adorn the front pages the next morning. Even the district council's flower arrangements, which had looked so fresh and colourful in the early part of the evening, were now wilting.

One Party stalwart, a middle-age lady, who was wearing a

'*Vote for Norma's Husband*' badge, said sadly: "He didn't deserve this . . . they didn't deserve this."

Looking tired, but without giving away any of the emotion he was feeling in his facial expressions, John shook the hands of all the other candidates, walked forward to the rostrum and began his acceptance speech by thanking Norma for her support. He said:

"Above all, I would like to thank Norma, perhaps these thanks are most appropriately expressed in private. Not only has she graced this constituency for 18 years, I think she has graced a much larger stage."

He paid tribute to the thousands of people who had worked and voted for him over the years in Huntingdonshire and said he was deeply privileged to have the opportunity of representing the constituency once more. He said:

"It is perfectly clear now that the Labour Party has had an extremely successful evening. I telephoned Mr Blair a little over an hour ago to congratulate him on his success and wish him every good fortune in the great responsibilities that he will have in the years that lie ahead. This is a great country, he inherits a country in extremely good economic strength. I wish him every success in sustaining that."

He ended by saying the Conservatives would listen to the voice of the electorate and consider the message the public had given them:

"We must reflect upon it. I know we will look to this day in the not too distant future, when my Party may once again return to govern in the service of this country."

John said afterwards that all campaigns in his constituency had been clean and open. He said:

"The people of Huntingdon don't like dirty politics. They don't like personality politics. They like to know what people are really like, what they care about and they make their own judgements, so some of the ugliness which was in the national campaign, some of the downright untruths that were spread, about pension policy for example, did not surface much in Huntingdon because the public did not have a great deal of interest in them. I went around the markets here and nobody raised those issues then. I got the same response I had had on previous occasions in less turbulent times. I don't think any of our opponents tried to make anything out of the national issues. Labour and the Liberals fought a clean campaign locally."

Norma, James and Elizabeth all travelled down to London with him afterwards. No-one slept. It was a difficult night. The family had been in the spotlight for so long, and now overnight they were yesterday's news. The country had a new Prime Minister, who was young, dynamic and extremely publicity friendly. Mr Blair, along with his wife and young children, happily went before the cameras the next day.

When John stood outside Downing Street on May 2 to announce his resignation, he said: "When the curtain falls, it is time to get off the stage and that is what I propose to do."

Then in attempt to lighten the intense atmosphere, he laughed, and said he was deliberately keeping his speech short so he could catch some cricket at The Oval.

On reflection, John says the election defeat was not as catastrophic than he had imagined. The Referendum vote was more damaging and tactical voting was more sophisticated than his Party had ever seen before. He said:

"I don't think the election campaign made much difference at all. The nation was pretty laid back about the whole thing. There were two or three incidents, which if you forgive me I won't elaborate on, that led me to believe that the electorate were of a settled mind and we didn't have enough votes. Lots of people who were solidly Conservative by instinct were saying: 'Is it safe to elect a Government for a fifth successive term?' 'Does that mean there's no opposition?' You could feel that all the way through."

102

THE PRIVATE MAJOR

But not all the Conservatives in Huntingdon had foreseen a Labour victory on May 1. Cyril Bridge was so convinced of his Party's success on polling day, he put some money on it. He said:

"I've read since that John knew we would lose, but I honestly thought we would pull it off. So much so, that I had a bet on it. A large bet a few weeks before and a smaller one on the day. If John knew we weren't going to win, I wish he told me . . . I could have saved myself a few bob."

STICKY WICKET

T HE day after the 1997 General Election, when the rest of the world, it seemed, was pontificating on the Tories' defeat, ex-Premier John Major took his seat at The Oval.

After his driver had handed back the keys to the official blue Prime Minister's Daimler, he and Norma jumped in the back of the chauffeur-driven Jaguar to which, as leader of the opposition, he was now entitled.

When they arrived at the cricket ground, accompanied by Elizabeth and James and their partners Luke and Elaine, John was immediately surrounded by a crowd of people, all wanting his autograph. One man handed him a copy of a national newspaper and asked him to sign it. The fellow cricket fan remarked: "You got a bit of a dodgy lbw decision last night, mate." John smiled and replied: "Yes, but the umpire's decision is final."

Dressed in a pale blue short sleeved shirt and wearing sunglasses, he spent the afternoon watching cricket. His refusal to give interviews or hold a post-mortem on the campaign and the huge loss of seats his Party had suffered the night before led to much speculation about his future.

Back in Huntingdon, constituency agent Peter Brown was running the gauntlet of emotional extremes. As well as his responsibilities to the MP, he is the fulcrum of the Conservative Party machine in the area and had to mastermind the Cambridgeshire County Council election campaign. The ruling Lib Dem/Labour alliance at Shire Hall looked vulnerable, and the Huntingdonshire area represented the Party's best hopes for returning to power. The county council elections were held alongside the Parliamentary one on May 1, but the count started the following day. The result was outstanding – Conservatives won three extra seats in his area, now holding 14 out of a possible 15, which meant the Party would be leading the county into the Millennium. It was a triumph which arrived after the General Election disaster and John's resignation, so the celebrations at the association headquarters in Archer's Court, Stukeley Road, Huntingdon, were rather subdued. For Peter, the punishing workload and events of the last 24 hours had turned it into: "a dreadful day." He said:

"We did what we set out to do in the county council elections, we swept the board. But, at the count, the news came through that The Boss was resigning and people were worried that he was leaving politics. I had to explain it was just the best thing for him to do, to stand aside and that he had lots more to contribute. But it took time for that to sink in. It was like a bereavement. Now there is plenty for the pair of them to do. They are still young. Norma, I'm sure, would like to write more books (her second, the history of Chequers, was published in 1996 and became a Christmas best-seller), while John still has a political career, more time for cricket and football and then other things, like his memoirs. The constituency and his work here still rank as his top priority."

During an interview with *The Hunts Post* on June 27, John said he had been "touched" by the sackfuls of letters he had received since the election – around 150,000 to date. Most were supportive and blamed his warring Party, rather than him personally, for the election defeat. He is in the process of replying, personally, to each of them, as well as the fifty-plus constituency letters he deals with every day and other correspondence.

After giving the matter some consideration, John feels the electorate's desire for change and some of the "excitements and exhilarations of the last few years" were the most damaging factors for his Party on May 1. He said:

"I say I had made up my mind before the election to resign as Party leader, but if the result had been close, then there would perhaps have been a compelling reason to stay on. There's a limited shelf life for politicians these days. The media is much more intrusive. The public see much more of politicians than they did before. It's impossible to turn on the news or open a newspaper without seeing what politicians are allegedly doing or saying and I think that shortens their shelf life.

"I don't think it was a practical proposition to stay on for another five years and if we had, every time something happened, people would harp back to 1990 and 1997. It was necessary, after 18 years, to have change. And in the interests of the Conservative Party, it was necessary to start again with some new faces.

"You can stand back and look again at where you are, what you do and what you stand for. I don't suggest you ditch all those things, it wouldn't work. People forget, over 10 million people voted for us. One has to look at some areas of policy, but by and large we have to look at new and younger faces. Many of the seats will come back comfortably. Many of the losses were the result of tactical voting . . . the result of [Sir James] Goldsmith and others."

He says he will "apportion blame later" for the election defeat, the strongest indication yet of his intention to name names in his memoirs, which he has already started planning. He sees his autobiography as a chance to put the record straight. He said:

"There are too many things which lie on the record inaccurately and need correcting, but I'm in no particular hurry."

He regards his efforts to win peace in Northern Ireland as one of his biggest achievements, and was disappointed not to be able to see it through to the end. But he is equally proud of the economic strength his Government created, saying:

"What mattered to me was public policy. That's why I was so

determined to get inflation down. All my life we've had this country damaged by inflation. At some stage, someone had to do something brutal and unpleasant, but it worked. It may have tossed out the Government that delivered it, but it has made us the best performing economy in Western Europe.

"When I became Prime Minister, we were heading for the worst recession for generations. We have come out of that recession with a sparkling economy and we did it with a tiny majority. We came very close to succeeding in Northern Ireland. Tony Blair has consulted me extensively on Northern Ireland and I think he is beginning to appreciate the nature of the people he's dealing with."

When John and Norma were thrust into the media spotlight after the 1990 Conservative leadership election, they found the experience daunting. They accepted the public interest in their lives, but couldn't understand why people wanted to mock.

In his first year of office, John would frantically search through the papers every morning looking for inaccuracies and misquotes. After a while, he learned to live with the less damaging stories and only became angry when he felt journalists had been grossly unfair or intrusive. He said:

"I tend not to dwell on it now, it's pointless. I was angry when stories about the children started to appear. By and large, they left Elizabeth alone, but with James they overstepped the mark with what they wrote on a number of occasions. Some of the stories in the Press were either invented or somebody lied to them. There were so many, it's almost impossible to draw them to my mind. On a number of occasions my views were expressed confidently by a so-called close friend, which was just utterly untrue. If I complained, they just said I was a public figure and they had every right to do it. It's best just to let it all drift past."

Of the personal sneering he says: "I've always upset the intellectuals who think I should have read some great book. I have learned what I have learned through my own experiences in life, not by reading somebody else's."

His Government did consider a privacy law to deal with

THE PRIVATE MAJOR

the excesses of the Press. He admitted:

"I couldn't find a way to draft a law that drew a distinction that wasn't a nonsense. That's why we have always fallen back on self regulation, because we simply couldn't frame a law that was sensible. In France they have laws, but it didn't stop what happened to Princess Diana, so I'm not in favour of legislation for dealing with the Press.

"It doesn't happen in the local or regional press, only in the competitive atmosphere of Fleet Street. The editors and the newspaper proprietors could stop it. If the worst excesses continue, then some Government at some time will legislate. How successful that will be, I have my doubts, but perhaps, just possibly they will take a greater grip themselves."

Since the election, John has had many offers of work, but still needs time to mull things over and make decisions about any long-term projects. He says he is in no hurry to decide and has plenty to do. Having already completed one lecture tour of America, he has invitations to speak until the end of 1999.

Many of his friends in Huntingdon believe that in time he will be regarded warmly by a wider public and judged fairly by the history books. Roger Juggins says:

"When history is written, people will see he had the hardest load of any Prime Minister this century.....and they didn't have the media to contend with. People say he should have kicked the rebels out, but if he had he would have had nothing left."

John has pledged to remain on the back benches "until I cease" and confirmed what most Conservatives in his constituency already knew, that Huntingdon is still home. He said:

"I wanted the job as MP for Huntingdon for a long time. I worked very hard to get it and pretty hard to keep it over the years and I shall go on doing it. I have worked 16 to 18 hours a day seven days a week since about 1987, and I hope things will slow down a bit now. I shall do some writing and speaking and continue to have constituency responsibilities and may even watch some more cricket. I will write an autobiography, but I need some time to think about it first."

At the Conservative Party Conference in October, he was given a prolonged standing ovation. As he stood on the platform with Norma, he told the audience they must back William Hague and unite to beat Labour.

He thanked the nation for the trust they had placed in successive Conservative Governments over the years and admitted he wished the events of May 1 had not been so severe. He said:

"As democrats we respect the electorate's decision and as politicians we must work to change it at the first available opportunity. Our election defeat was not your election defeat. Rather than brood over it, we must accept our defeat as gracefully as we can. We shouldn't waste time on pointless recriminations.

"We should go out in the towns and the cities and the villages and begin to build for the future of the next Conservative Government.

"It's a simply choice – back William Hague, rediscover the art of working together, fight every seat, for every vote or fight one another and lose elections. It will be difficult being the leader of a newly defeated party. For a while people won't listen to what we have to say. But that will pass. The tide will turn and as the local election results are already suggesting, perhaps more speedily than anyone imagines.

"Remember that our party has served the country in Government more often and longer and better than any democratic party in the whole history of politics. At the end of this week, there is one message that I long to hear from the conference: we are the Conservative Party, we exist to serve a nation that is conservative by instinct and we will be back."

Conservatives supporters stamped their feet and cheered at the end of that speech, and kept it up as he left the room.

As he stood down from the platform, with applause still ringing in his ears, he would not have had time to reflect on his meteoric rise to the top job.

He would have not given a second thought to a damp November evening in 1976 when he walked from a much smaller stage in front of a much smaller audience in Huntingdon after being chosen to represent the constituency for his Party.

The people of the Huntingdon Conservative Association who put their faith in John Major, the banker from Brixton, that night were confident they had selected the right man. Their belief in the man, his qualities and his convictions has never wavered. John Bridge said:

"I see no end to him continuing as Huntingdon's MP, but he would not wish to outstay his welcome, although that will never go from Huntingdon because the people have such an affinity with him. I feel now he has the opportunity to reap some of the benefits of his hard work. I don't think anybody really understands the kind of pressures and the all-consuming way that being Prime Minister takes over your life. As far as I know his commitment is here. We've chatted and he has said 'please tell me when the time is right for me to go.'"